Azure Savage

You Failed Us

Cover images shot by Michael B. Maine

Printed by Lulu Press Inc.

Published by Azure Savage
Email: azure@owensavage.com

Dedicated to all the students of color, past and present, who have not been heard. I hear you.

Acknowledgments:

I wouldn't have been able to make this book a reality without the support of many. Thank you to Foundry10 for sponsoring me to finish this book, and giving me resources to make my dream a reality. Thank you to all the students of color who allowed me to interview them, and trusted me with their stories. Thank you to my mentors across the different organizations I am part of; shout-outs to G.G. Silverman, Reagan Jackson, Michael B. Maine, and Rebecca Milliman. Whether or not you helped me directly with this book, your overall support means so much to me and has kept me going through tough times. Thank you to the Youth Undoing Institutionalized Racism for providing me with the most important education I will ever receive. Thank you to my mom and my dad for keeping it real with me, and always being there. Thank you to my pups for being adorable and unconditionally loving me. Thank you to my friends for cheering me along throughout this process.

Finally, thank you to all my black, transgender siblings. You inspire me with your resilience and determination to live as you choose despite the hate that we face. I am proud to be in a community with you.

Contents

Includes topics of sexual assault, disordered eating, self harm, and suicide.

Introduction

When I was in elementary school, every year my teacher took individual pictures of all the children in the class and then hung the pictures on the wall. I always refused to have my picture taken. I was the only black student in my class every year, and I constantly noticed the differences between me and the other students. I didn't want everyone who walked into the room and looked at the wall of pictures to notice that I was different too. I would rather them think that the class had no black students than for me to be the only one; I wanted to be invisible. As much as my teachers begged me, got irritated with me, or even called my mom, my picture never made it up on the wall alongside the smiling faces of the rest of my class.

My story as a black student attending schools within Seattle begins in kindergarten. Now, as a high school student, I have firsthand experience with the current education system and the issues within it. After years of watching and receiving harm from school, and then comprehending the way racism is institutionalized within schools, I needed to say something about it, and this book is my "something." I started this project with a plan to interview students of color from different schools in the Seattle area, and give them a place to be heard. As I've been writing this book over the last year and a half, it's become more than that. I originally wanted to only include other people's experiences, but I've come to realize that the most important subject for me to write about is myself. Digging within my own past to pull out and reflect on memories was challenging, but necessary to honestly share my story. I go beyond just what I experienced in school as a black student; I want to share how what I've been through has shaped who I am and the way I've navigated life and the education system.

I chose to base this book solely off of individual experiences. I use the insight I gained from them, the racial analysis I've learned over the last few years to illustrate the racism found within schools. Experiences are often dismissed as personal issues when they should be addressed to understand the big picture issues, examine the cause of them, and work to improve them. I tremendously appreciate all the students who allowed me to interview them, for supporting this project, and being open with me. Because these stories are personal, and I was asked by several people to keep their identities anonymous, I've chosen to keep all names private. The quotes from these students are featured in every chapter alongside my own stories and my analysis. As I interviewed people, listened to the recordings, and pulled quotes, I found common threads throughout them, and each became a topic that I focus on in a chapter.

I've dreamt of this book being many things. I want it to be a wake-up call to Seattle, and the rest of the country, that we need to make changes now to improve the experiences of students of color. I want teachers reading this to reevaluate their pedagogy and work to make their classes a space for all students to learn and be supported. I want white students to read this and act to be advocates for their peers. I want students of color, past and present, reading this to know their experiences matter. If anything, I hope this book makes everyone reading it feel something. Whether that be anger, sadness, guilt, or anything else that comes up, I hope that you allow yourself to be with that emotion. Let yourself take that feeling and really, truly feel it. Writing this book forced me to sit with my own emotions, even when they caused me pain. From the anger I feel for the students who have been held down by their own schools, to the hope I cling on to, and to the shame that has long been trapped inside me, getting myself to accept these emotions helped me find a deeper connection to the experiences that other students of color and I have had. I hope that the emotions and vulnerability I've poured into this work allows you to have a deeper connection as well.

Segregation

I didn't know a single student outside the honors program until middle school. At my elementary school we had honors classes and general classes. The honors program requires students to pass a placement test to enter, while the general program is open to anyone. They were two different worlds, taught by different teachers, held in different classrooms, and serving different students. I went entire days without having a single interaction with someone outside my program; it was like running into someone from a completely different school. The programs were racially segregated; general classes had black kids, and honors classes had white kids.

Keeping the programs meticulously separate had many downsides. Personally, it was nearly impossible to interact with and befriend other black kids. It seemed wrong to try simply because of how hard it was. The programs were cleanly split into black and white which reinforced the social boundaries I had already been exposed to. Figuring out where I fit in was made harder by the racial segregation. I knew I was not white, but I was in the white program.

It made it impossible to connect with my blackness because I was not in the right program to be black. I was forced to cling onto my whiteness and let go of my blackness as a means of survival in my classes, all at the age of six.

I went to that school for four years and didn't make one friend outside of my program. Because I was in the white program, whiteness surrounded my days at school. White friends, white teachers, white classmates— it was all I knew. I only had two black friends during elementary school: one in first and second grade, and one in fifth grade; both of them were in honors too, and the only other black girls. I've made a lot of progress connecting with other black students in high school, yet still the way I interact in the black community today is heavily impacted by my lack of black peers and friends at a young age.

I had to internalize a lot about racism and what white people thought of me because of how loudly the people in my program talked about people in the general program. It was clear that they viewed themselves as superior; possibly because parents would praise them for being extra smart, possibly because they were white. It was an ongoing joke that kids in the general program were crazy and people in my classes saw them as much different from themselves. Honors kids would say things about how loud, annoying and dumb they were. At the time, I was aware that kids in the general program were black, and honors kids were white, but I didn't connect these comments with the racial implications. I cannot say certainly that these comments were intentionally racist, but I also believe that racism was a factor.

History books teach us that schools were desegregated because of the Supreme Court case "Brown v. Board of Education." This happened in 1954, yet today, schools are carrying out a new kind of segregation. Even though schools are integrated, after a brief look at who's in what class anyone could conclude segregation still exists. Black students and other minorities are found in the lower level classes while white students and Asian students are found in classes taught at a higher level.

My high school is around thirty percent black, yet I was the only black student in my AP chemistry class. For those who aren't familiar, AP stands for "Advanced Placement" and are college level classes taught in high school that can be transferred into college credit if a student pays for and passes the standardized test near the end of the year. In any approximately thirty-person class, if around thirty percent of the school is black, I would expect to see ten black students. However, only three percent of my class was black, and I was the three percent. Say that this was an issue with only that class, and the four other AP chemistry classes had a proportional number of black students. But it wasn't only in this class. I was one of two black students in the period I was in first semester, I switched halfway through the year, and if I had been in any other AP chemistry class I still would've been one out of two black students or the only one.

A person looking for the simplest answer may conclude that black students are just not interested in AP chemistry, but this is only making a generalization, and black students are individuals who can be interested in anything. And, I was interested in the class, and a few other black students were, so clearly that's not the case. The truth is that black students are discouraged from taking advanced level courses, by their peers, teachers, or even by their own socialized ideas of who should take that class. Black and brown students are influenced by the people they see in that class, who are predominantly white and Asian, and make an assessment: they aren't meant to be there. When talking about segregation within classes, East Asian students tend to fall more with the white students. In this area of academia, they have a similar privilege to white students.

When I was entering my Freshman year, my high school was implementing a new strategy to integrate the honors program. It was called "honors for all," and as the name suggests, it put all freshmen students in honors classes despite the program they were in during middle school. When people heard that the school was doing this, there were mixed opinions. Many parents of students who had been in honors for years expressed their concerns. In summary, they believed it was unfair for their children to be subjected to this because they were "gifted" and deserved to have a separate program. It was clear that their reasoning was racist. The program was "honors for all," not "honors for no one." Their children would still be in the same program they had been in, but would be joined by students who hadn't had the opportunity to be in it previously. Even with the backlash, the program was going to happen.

Because of this new strategy, my freshman year honors classes were very diverse. It was a big improvement to look around my class and not only see white faces. There was some tension between people who had come from different programs, but overall, it seemed to be an effective strategy for integration, until I started to notice the holes within the plan. Starting sophomore year, it is up to the students whether to take honors classes, AP classes, or neither. In addition, freshman who had been in honors during middle school are placed in math and science classes one or two years ahead of those who were not. Freshman coming from honors are in Pre-Calculus while those from general are in Algebra because people in the honors program are placed in eighth grade level math, sometimes Algebra, in sixth grade, putting them two years ahead from the start of middle school. The same applies to science. Unsurprisingly to me, sophomore year the honors classes were back to the way they were before: white and Asian. Those ahead in math and science were able to start taking AP science and math classes sophomore year while others could start later. The strategy worked well for freshman year history and language arts because it was mandated, however once students were given a choice while being influenced by what their friends were going to sign up for, what their teachers and counselors recommended, and how well they did freshman year, the programs returned to their previously segregated status. It was a shame to watch how the attempt failed in the long run, but I didn't expect it to succeed without a continuation plan into the next three years.

"I came from the Philippines, but I spoke English. I went into the ELL (English Language Learners) program, even though I could speak English. I was put into that because I flowed with the other immigrant kids. ELL classes are sad, they don't get a lot of funding. I was there with a bunch of black and brown kids, there's not many white kids, and we always had this strange white teacher who speaks maybe Spanish but

no other language. They're always the weird ones, I remember we had to massage my ELL teacher's back. During it I thought it was a weird experience, but over time I heard news stories about how the ELL program was harmful to students. Every ELL classroom I've been in has been barren, no posters, no windows, it's like a prison cell. There's a lot of people who were stuck in that system."

"In elective classes there's an actual equal ratio of people of color to white people. In my marketing class, there are more students of color than white students. In honors pre-calculus class, there's not a single black student, it's all white kids and Asian students. From my experience, the teacher assumes the class will be rowdy if the class is all people of color. If it's a majority white class you're expected to be more respectful and attentive in class, even just a better student overall. My math teacher has said that she expects better behavior from us than students who aren't in honors. It's annoying, just because they're in a different learning level doesn't mean she should treat them differently."

Other programs exist at most high schools, such as the ELL program, and individualized education. They're built for students who have different needs or abilities than the rest of the students.

I'm not going to get into either because I don't have experience in them myself, and was unable to get enough students who were willing to be interviewed, so it's not my place to speak on. I want to acknowledge that not having these students represented in my book is one of its flaws, and the students of color in these programs have been marginalized in different ways through the intersection of their identities. Aside from those programs, honors, AP, and general classes, another category of classes are those that aren't split into general or advanced, usually these classes are electives, such as languages or art. It's interesting to look at the difference in racial makeup between all these types of classes. From my own experience, these classes are some of the most racially diverse. My elective classes always had more black students than any of my honors classes. I always liked my elective classes more because of this exact reason; I was able to interact with black people who I wouldn't have met in any of my other classes, and the environment was way less white. These classes felt like a breath of fresh air in between the rest of my suffocating class schedule.

Teachers teach differently and expect different things from different class levels. When there is a strong correlation between class level and race, I can infer that they are treating students differently because of their race, not only the class level they are in. Black students are not only directed towards a lower level class, they are directed towards teachers who look down on those classes because of the racial makeup. I've had teachers who teach both honors classes and general classes, and I always signed up for honors classes because I've been in the honors program for years. It's disappointing to me how many times my teachers have compared my class to the non-honors ones they teach, and make comments like "you guys are much more behaved" or "I always dread my fourth period class because I don't know how to control them." These comments are clearly rooted in stereotypes and are disrespectful to the students in the other classes. I think it's wrong to be talking shit about them because it always will circulate around until people in that class are told. It's the teacher's job to handle their class, and if they are only comfortable with white students, they shouldn't be teaching.

> *"My school is surprisingly diverse. There's a substantial population of people of color, but it's still majority white. It's very interesting in that way because there's a lot of different kinds of people, but the more segregated aspect of it is the IB (International Baccalaureate) program. Even though they say the program is open to everyone, and anyone can take IB classes, it really is a matter of whether your parents are aware of the program and support you being in high academics. At the surface it looks diverse, but there's a lot of under the surface segregation."*

Segregation in schools is subtle enough to remain in place, yet incredibly obvious after someone points it out, and I can point out segregation in different forms throughout my high school. I see self-segregation especially in where people hang out. At my school, there are two distinct areas that somehow have become tied to racial groups. The courtyard on the side of the school, and the balcony above the cafeteria. Everyone at the school is aware that the white students hang out in the courtyard, and the black students hang out on the balcony. It's surprising to see a group of white students on the balcony, and rare for black students to hang out in the courtyard. I have no idea how it came to be this way, or why, but during the time I've gone to the school it's always been that way. As someone who's been friends with people from both the "white side" and the "black side" of the school, I felt comfortable hanging out in either area, but I know people who refuse to go to one or the other.

Structured segregation is set up to keep black and brown students from making up a large portion of advanced classes. Someone may suggest, "Well, it's their fault for choosing to not be in an advanced class!" Again, this is a simple answer to a complex issue. Segregation of programs isn't a personal issue of black students, it's a structural problem in our society that is intentional, not an unfortunate coincidence. There are many factors as to why black students tend to not take advanced classes, including lack of support, being uninformed, or being persuaded to take a lower level class. Blaming the student's choice overlooks the reason that they made the choice.

> *"The majority of students in my honors and AP classes are white or white passing, while my non-honors and non-AP classes have mostly people of color. My school's student population is majority students of color which is confusing because my advanced classes don't reflect that. As an Asian person, I have more privilege than other people of color. There are people like me in my advanced*

classes, but not other people of color."

As I briefly touched on, segregation of schools doesn't impact all students of color equally. Even though Asian students face other inequities within education, being placed in lower level classes is not one of them. It's also not only an issue of black and brown students not being in advanced classes, it's the fact that they make up the population of most general classes. The imbalance goes both ways, not enough students of color in advanced classes and too many in general classes.

The students of color who are in advanced classes are usually the ones closest to whiteness. I know that a big reason I was in the program was because I'm mixed race with a white mother. Since my mom is white and middle class, she knew about the program years before I tested into it, and always planned for me to be in it. I wasn't one of the people who paid to take the test multiple times, I got in on the first try, but still, having my mom be aware of the program and having her support gave me an advantage that other students of color don't have. Throughout my years in honors, the few other students of color were Asian students, especially ones mixed with white, and the few other black students also happened to be mixed with only a few exceptions. Students with at least one white parent are more likely to hear about the program in the first place and can afford to pay for their child to take the test until they pass.

"When I got to the school in ninth grade
I was in the honors track for freshman.
Basically, we were completely cut off from all
the other freshman. There was us, the honors

track, and there was the regular education track. Even though we were getting incredible academics, it was isolating for me. I was the only black person in the entire program."

"The AP and honors classes have more white and Asian students while the general and elective classes have more students of color. My school is majority students of color, but in my AP and honors classes it's at most five students of color, and maybe two or three black students."

Students of color who choose to take advanced classes are making a tradeoff. In exchange for a good education and a higher chance of getting into college, they give up their support system and isolate themselves from students who look like them. This is a common thread in the lives of students of color. It's easy for some to look down on giving up the opportunity for a higher level of education because of not having friends in the class, but that view implies that all students of color only care about friends and not their education, which is not true. It's more than having someone to laugh with during class; it's the advantage of having someone to ask for help on homework, to study for the test with, to stand up for you, to confront the racist teacher with. The support that comes from having friends in a class is something that I see white students take for granted. It puts students of color in a severe disadvantage because they have less support to help them succeed.

"At my school, there aren't many white people. I don't see much segregation, it's very mixed. White students almost have a disadvantage at my school because they are the minority, which is interesting to me since it's so rare. My school doesn't do the typical honors class system anymore. You can decide if you want to opt into honor or opt out, but everyone is in the same class."

Advanced classes do not have to be segregated the way that they often are. However, desegregating them does not have an obvious solution. The only way to move towards equity is for the honors program that starts in kindergarten to be dismantled. When I went to visit my elementary school five years after I finished fifth grade, I heard a similar narrative to mine from the current students; the programs were still as segregated as they were when I attended the school. It did not seem like progress has been made in diversifying the programs. Having honors classes in high school seems reasonable if the goal is for interested students to take them for the challenge, but the current goal is to give already privileged students even more of an advantage. The fact that many white kids have never even considered a general level class shows that they view advanced classes as their default. The system that tracks students in either honors or general from the time they're six years old makes fixing the inequities in high school impossible.

Dismantling the program is easier said than done. Based off the white parent backlash due to "honors for all," I don't think that white parents would be thrilled to hear that their "exceptionally bright" children will be in the same program as everyone else. It's important to take into account which parents are providing the school with donations, and where those donations are going. If white parents are giving large sums of money to the school, they would want it to directly improve the classes that their students are in. Black kids are either lumped into classrooms that are less important to the school, or placed into classrooms where they are isolated. The white kids get the better end of the deal. Usually, they get to be in the classes they want with their friends and a teacher that supports them. The few white kids who are in general classes don't have to experience the same racism that black students in general classes do.

Segregation, like racism, is often shrugged off as something that happened only in the past. However, segregation, and the people who benefit from it, have adapted to today's society and still thrive. Even though it may not be as explicit as it was in the past, its existence in Seattle schools is obvious. We cannot say everyone is receiving equal education when racial segregation in schools is giving a better education to white and Asian students than to their black and brown peers. The act of putting everyone in the same building does not effectively end segregation and promote equity of education when classrooms are continuing to be divided by race.

Isolation

I ate my lunch alone in the bathroom for the first time in seventh grade. For my thirteen-year-old self, this was hitting bottom. I was entirely isolated from everyone at my school, so my last resort was to spend some quality time with the plumbing system. I usually sat with some of the eighth graders from my math class that had been nice to me. Unfortunately, all of them were gone on that one day for the eighth-grade field trip, a day that I had been dreading for weeks. It was thirty minutes of pure hell and anxiety. I was terrified that people would walk in and laugh at me. I could barely eat my food because of the disgusting smells and nauseating way my inner thoughts were spiraling in on me. I locked myself in a stall and screamed into my backpack while tears flowed down my face.

In this moment, I hated myself. I hated that I was in this position; I hadn't been able to establish any solid friendships that year, and that there was nothing I could do except wait for the time to pass. The year before, in sixth grade, I had friends. Not only that, I was in the so-called "popular" group in my grade. During that time, I had a white best friend, and we were both fascinated with the concept of popularity. The importance of popularity was extremely emphasized in our friendship, and made me believe that being popular was the only way to be important. I let this get to me, and fully believed it. I should've seen it coming when that friend left me for friends who would keep her at the top of the middle school social hierarchy. After we stopped being friends, I fell into depression for the first time. I could feel myself becoming my own definition of a loser. I was the person that she and I used to make fun of; I was friendless, unpopular, and irrelevant. Looking at myself with that lens started to manifest a deep shame within myself that made me feel like I was never going to be anyone.

Sitting alone in the bathroom was better than sitting alone at the lunch table for everyone to see, but it still made see myself as a typical social outcast. I've always been dramatic, but I was still in a lot of legitimate pain during this time. It's genuinely hard for me to recall much from that year because of the way my brain has slowly diluted the painful memories with fog. To put into perspective my mindset from when I was thirteen, here's a section from my diary:

> *"It's the first Saturday night of 7th grade and I already hate it. I hate my classes, I hate being there. School absolutely sucks. I hate being forced to prepare for a life I don't give a fuck about. I need help. But no one will ever understand what I'm going through. It's not just a suicidal teen problem. Everything I know hurts me. It breaks me apart. My mind used to be my favorite place to be, but now*

that's not even true anymore. I need to get on with my life but I'm stuck. I have nowhere to go and nowhere to go back to. I'm afraid that this is forever. I don't want to be alone. I have no friends. I have no one who cares. I want to leave this girl behind and become the person-or-whatever I was meant to be."

I don't know anyone who would say they enjoyed seventh grade, but for me it stands out as one of the most isolated periods of my life. By that I mean, I genuinely had no real friends. Even though I usually had people to sit with at lunch, and people to talk to in class, I had no one to talk to about important things, and no one to tell how much pain I was in. Being thirteen and trying to figure out who you are is rough as it is, and having no one I felt I could open to made it worse. Leaving behind my childhood, but still not having anyone to help me transition into my teenage years was challenging. I was realizing that I wasn't who I wanted to be and not knowing what that meant, so I spent most of my time outside of school sitting alone with my thoughts, worries, and fears because I felt like I had no one else to share them with. I recognize this year as the time my mental health took a turn for the worse which continued to affect me for years to come. It was hard to not look at my position as something that I deserved, and it felt like something must be wrong with me.

Everyone can likely recall a time in their lives where they felt disconnected from other people. I've found myself isolated in my life the most during school. Isolation can happen when students of color can't find a place for themselves to fit in, and have little connection with other students. It can occur in different ways; being isolated from all other students, and being isolated from other students of color are both types of isolation. People also feel isolated even if they have people around them because they might not feel connected to those people or feel comfortable being vulnerable. Isolation has come up for me in different ways and different intensities throughout my time in school.

"Freshman year, even still a little bit now, there were only white girls in my friend group. I came from a private school, so I think I just gravitated to them because they were what I was used to. There were so many microaggressions, and people obsessed with smooth hair and skin. It felt like I had a mask on until I got home. I was friends with a lot of white people and put myself in those environments as a means of survival."

White friend groups have a strong effect on students of color, even if they are supportive and healthy friendships. It's important for us to be able to have connections with other students of color, and if those connections are weak or nonexistent, it poses challenges. For one, students of color experience racism that white students can't ever fully understand, even if they do empathize with it. It's vital to be able to have other people to talk to about racism, be able to rant about experiences, and laugh at the foolery of white people with. Some white people are open to criticism of whiteness and racism, however, it is more common for them to be uncomfortable with it. Whether they get defensive of themselves, provide only sympathy, or try to end the conversation before it begins, white students are generally not a good resource for students of color to process to racism that they experience.

The white girl friend groups I've been in had interesting dynamics with race. Living in Seattle, where liberalism and "wokeness" are widely accepted and taken on by the white community, they did everything they could to show they weren't racist while simultaneously feeding into racism. One group specifically stands out, the group I was friends with in eighth grade and freshman year. The way they fetishized black men, used the n-word, stole the style of black girls by wearing hoops and braids, and made me feel less than them, while acting like they were the most woke people in the world, was ridiculous. One of them said, "I wish I was black," completely seriously. When I was in it, I didn't feel comfortable at all bringing up their problematic tendencies, but looking back I'm amazed at everything I used to let slide.

I reason that my silence came from two different factors. The first was that being isolated as one of the two black girls associated with that friend group made me feel powerless; I was outnumbered. If they couldn't see the fault in their actions themselves, especially since they claimed "wokeness," I doubted that I would be able to show them. I also was far less sure of myself when it came to discussing race than I am now, mainly because I was still somewhat ignorant about racial issues and hadn't developed the language to talk about it. If I could only go back in time, with the knowledge, confidence, and awareness that I have now, I probably could have shut it down immediately and got the fuck out of the friend group.

The second one was harder for me to realize; my horrible experiences with complete isolation from all students at my school made me terrified about losing them. Even freshman year, some of the shame around being unpopular was still prevalent in my mindset. Whenever I considered leaving the group, I remembered that they were one of the most popular groups in my grade, and I didn't want to let go of that status. Thinking about that now, I realize that I was completely misguided and my priorities in friendship were warped, but that was where I was at. I would've rather been isolated within a popular friend group than be isolated completely on my own. Still, I was experiencing isolation that disconnected me from people who looked like me. This impacted my self-worth, my identity, and the way that I treated myself. I was simultaneously proud of myself for having friends, but being harmed because they were all white.

After I was no longer friends with them and had taken some time to reflect, I realized how tokenized I was in the group. They were all aware that I was the token black friend, and made jokes about it all the time. I feel like they exploited my identity to prove that they weren't racist, so that they could feel better about themselves and create the image that they wanted. I got asked, "I'm not racist, right?" constantly.

"I'm a privileged person in some ways, and I get told I'm like a 'white' black person. That made it hard to be friends with other

black and brown people. I felt like there was a weird divide. It took me a long time to find these people to be friends with. Still working on it. For a long time, I didn't have any friends of color, so I didn't know how to establish those relationships."

"It was difficult to have a relationship with other black students at my school when I was isolated from most of them. I went to a Black Student Union meeting and I immediately noticed how there was a relationship between the other people there that I felt I didn't have and that I was afraid I'd never be able to develop. I should've worked harder at trying to make more black friends and more friends of color because there were times when I really did need them, and I didn't have them. I didn't go to Black Student Union enough to build those relationships of support. That's something I'm working on doing now, but I wish I'd been able to do it last year."

"Most of the people of color who I attend high school with have gone to school with other people of color their whole lives, so it doesn't even faze them. For me, it's very hard to find people who have experienced what I have. In the beginning of the school year, I first realized that being displaced from the other students of color was a

thing. As the year has gone on, and I've been in the same classes for a while, I've realized that people in the classes I take have 'groups' and I'm not really in any of them."

Being isolated from other students of color, whether it's because of the classes we're in or the friendships we have, makes it difficult to reach out and find a community of color at our schools. Especially for those who have been isolated for long periods of time, we can feel doubtful about whether we will be wanted in that space. For most of my life up until high school, I had been in exclusively white spaces. With my mom being white, being in the honors program, and being involved in swim team and drama, white people consumed my whole life. I wanted to have friends who weren't white, and find out more about black culture. I wanted to see who I could be if I fully embraced my blackness and surrounded myself with other black people. Even though I wanted to do all of this, I had no idea how to get from point A to point B. I had this goal of having black friends and being around more students of color, but there isn't a written-out guide I could follow. I had to create the journey on my own which seemed impossible.

One person who really pushed this on me was my boyfriend from freshman and sophomore year. Our relationship had many flaws, and I'm very grateful that it ended when it did, but I recognize that he was the person who made me understand that I really needed to have black friends. He was a black basketball player, and being around him made me want to explore more of my black culture because of how cultured he was. He immediately noticed how whitewashed I was as we got to know each other, and made me feel horrible about it. In some ways, he shamed me into feeling like I wasn't valid as a black person unless I changed who I was. He often made fun of me for being too white which was hurtful and made me insecure about my identity, but I'm glad he pushed me. Eventually, that shame and insecurity started to shift into an even stronger desire to find black friends and educate myself on black culture.

Part of what he laughed at me about was my lack of knowledge on mainstream black American culture. I hadn't watched any of the iconic movies or TV shows, hadn't listened to much rap or hip hop, and didn't know a lot of the cultural icons. It made me feel really embarrassed to know nothing about my own culture because I grew up being surrounded by whiteness. I knew it wasn't my fault that as a child I hadn't known to ask for a more culturally diverse upbringing, but I felt like it was now my job to make up for the years of isolation from black culture that I faced. Even though I was now hyper aware of the ignorance I had of my own culture, I had no idea how to connect to it. I watched all the movies he told me about, incorporated rap music into what I listened to, and researched any person I didn't know about. It took me a while to realize that no matter how many movies I watched, the real education would be from immersing myself in black spaces.

My boyfriend and I broke up at the end of sophomore year. During our relationship, he was my only friend, and more importantly, the only black person I spent time with. I realized that if I didn't act on it, I would end back up isolated in white friend groups, or be completely isolated from everyone. I started going out of my way at school to find black spaces. I was worried that they would think I was uptight and rude because I had been in honors for so long. I desperately wanted them to know that I hated being in the program, and wouldn't have been in it if I saw the racism when I was six. Once I started interacting and building relationships with more students of color, I realized that if anything, they felt bad for me, and had the assumption that I had been fully whitewashed. I admitted that yes, I've been whitewashed, but I want to snap out of it and figure out who I really am. I found out quickly that other students of color had nothing against me, and wanted to be friends too. They didn't even laugh at me, except at my dancing, the way my ex-boyfriend had because they understood it wasn't my fault that I was put in white spaces, including the honors program, at a young age. The more I spent time in spaces of color, the more I realized what I had been missing this whole time. It felt natural to be friends with these people, to trust them, and to surround myself with them.

> *"In my English and History classes I'm supposed to be the spokesperson for black literature and black history. It's awkward cause I don't want to speak on every black person's experiences, but I also don't want my white teacher to take a leadership role in the discussion. I feel isolated in terms of people understanding what I'm talking about. If you don't have support from teachers and classmates, it feels like you're struggling through it by yourself. Also, if there aren't any other students of color in the class, I get uncomfortable. It makes me feel like I'm constantly stressed, and I have no one to confide in."*

"I went to a private school the beginning of freshman year. Black kids were basically on our own cause we would only talk to each other. So, when I went to my honors classes, there were only white people who have been in private schools all their lives. They all knew each other, so I would just be sitting there, all alone. I did not talk to anybody."

Being the only person of color in a room brings a lot of pressure and discomfort. In some classes, like history and literature classes, we are looked on to be a resource for any race related question, but not for anything else. It's a burden to feel like we must be a representative for our entire racial group even though all we can truly speak on is our own opinions and experiences. Not knowing anyone else in a class makes it harder because of the lack of support and established connections, especially when they are sharing notes, studying together, and updating each other when we aren't able to do that alone. It gives white students another advantage because in white dominated classes, they will likely know someone, and even if they don't, it's easier for them to connect with their white peers.

I've noticed that in a white dominated classroom with only a couple students of color, we tend to self-segregate and isolate together throughout the class even if we didn't know each other previously. I met one of my best friends this way; I transferred to a class second semester where they were the only brown student, and they immediately introduced themselves and started a conversation when I walked in. They seemed ecstatic that they were finally not the only student of color in the class. I'd heard of them before, but never met them, and only a few days into the class we were already connecting and building a relationship. We always tried to find a way to sit by each other and work together because the rest of the class acted as if we were a joke. There's something about struggling together with someone that creates such a strong bond.

> *"Last year, I didn't really know any Filipino people in my grade. There were only a few upperclassmen who I knew of. It doesn't seem like there are very many Filipino kids at school which is sad because I don't have many friends who are like me and I feel isolated."*

Not knowing where to find your community at your school is an issue for many of us. Sometimes schools have small populations of certain ethnicities, or don't have any clubs or activities meant to bring these students together. The goal isn't necessarily to only hang out with people from our background. I think it's important to be able to interact with and be around all types of people, but it's beneficial for there to be spaces for certain groups of students to collectivize, get to know each other, and be able to create a safe space for each other. Knowing that there are other students at our schools who can relate to us validates our experiences and provides a support system.

There are ways that our experiences in classes can be improved by those with the power and privilege to do so. I believe that teachers need to play a strong role in supporting people of color who are alone in their classes. Simple things like assigning seats on the first day, so no one sits alone, and checking to make sure no one is being left out in discussions can make a difference. Still, more needs to be done to prevent students of color from being isolated in white classes which starts with dismantling the tracking system, and changing the norms around who takes advanced classes. In schools where the population of students of color is low, teachers must work even harder to keep those students involved and comfortable in classes. White students also need to play a role in improvements. Acknowledging their privilege is the first step, and then they should use their privilege to help their peers. They should include students of color in their classes without tokenizing their identities, meaning including us only to prove they aren't racist, or only for race related questions. Inclusion should happen by inviting them into discussions, asking them if they want to work together, and educating their white peers when they are contributing to the isolation.

Within schools, there needs to be a stronger effort from the faculty to create safe spaces for students of color to be able to connect with each other. I believe that this should start in at least middle school because that's when a lot of students experience the most isolation, and overall middle school is absolute hell. Even if these places exist, more effort is needed to inform students. I never knew where to find a space to be with other students of color, and since I was in all white classrooms, there was no one to ask. Like I said, there's not a written-out guide on how to make friends of color and find that essential support. We deserve guidance to help us out on whatever journey we're on to get us to a place where we feel supported and valued.

Different

One day when I was in second grade I looked down at my thighs to see how much they covered my desk seat, and compared it to the other girls in the class who were all white. I concluded from this observation that I was fat because of how I compared to the white girls. It didn't help that a year later, when I was in third grade, I started puberty. My body developed much sooner than my peers which made me incredibly insecure and dysphoric. From what I had learned from media, my friends, and my mom, being skinny was important. I was always the only black girl and the biggest girl in my class which, along with the way my body was changing, made me despise being in the body that I was in. This self-hatred started to manifest in different ways, including restricting my eating and forcing myself to throw up. I was ten years old when this started. I desperately wanted to fit into the same clothes as my friends fit into, and I felt embarrassed if I finished all my food and they still had food on their plate. I made up excuses for the way that I looked so I would not be labeled as fat. I brushed it off as having "big bones."

When my eating disorder started to take over at the beginning of fifth grade, I made a journal to track my progress. I would write down everything I ate, and whether I purged it. The goal was always to stay under a certain number of calories a day which I'm sure was scarily low, so any excess food would have to be purged. I would weigh myself every day to make sure that the number consistently went down. I can still picture one specific page from this book in my head; it was a countdown to my birthday which gave me one month to lose a certain amount of weight. At some point, my mom found this journal, and the shame I felt from her seeing it made me rethink everything and eventually stop the behavior, while the mindset I had stayed the same.

Throughout fourth and fifth grade I was on a swim team, but I didn't start swimming at an intense and competitive level until the end of fifth grade. I practiced up to fifteen hours a week which meant I needed to eat a lot of food for the amount I was exercising. I was the most physically fit that I've ever been, the only time I ever had and likely ever will have a six pack. Still, even though I was working my ass off in the pool every day, I thought that I was fat and unhealthy. All of this was because of a new trend that was at full force: the thigh gap. I'm so glad this trend has faded with time, but as a reminder it was a trend that defined a "perfect body" by the presence of a gap between the thighs when the feet were touching. Such a strange beauty standard! At this time, I had no idea how unnecessary and unrealistic this gap was, and I would check how much my thighs touched every single day. I was absolutely obsessed with achieving a thigh gap which triggered a second wave of my eating disorder.

It felt like everything around me was consumed by the thigh gap, from social media, to my friends talking about it, the way I compared myself to everyone. My best friend and I, the same one who would ditch me a few months later, had a plan to both get thigh gaps by not eating lunch, exercising during P.E. class, measuring ourselves, and filling each other in on our progress. I was so hungry every day after swim practice, not having eaten since breakfast, and finally got home only to feel ashamed to eat any more than one serving of dinner. I felt weak and dizzy all the time, but I was desperate for a thigh gap. I swam on an empty stomach for months which was dreadful. I wasn't performing well in meets because my body wasn't getting enough fuel to work as hard as I wanted it to. Eventually, the internet craze around the thigh gap had died down, and I was able to stop focusing on it. It still rang in the back of my head, and I still hated the way my body looked. Despite this, I started eating more again, and listening to my body. My swim times started to drop, and I saw the positive effect that eating enough had. For a moment, I was at peace with my weight and with my eating habits.

Things started to change for the worse when I quit swimming in the beginning of seventh grade, and until junior year, I consistently was putting on weight. During this time, I moved from being isolated on my own, to again being isolated in white friend groups which caused me to continue comparing myself to them the way I'd been comparing myself to white girls my whole life. I fell back into my old habits and started dieting and restricting. As I noticed I was gaining weight, I would try out everything possible to lose weight, but was never consistent and continued to gain. My first two years of high school were consumed with different diets that warped my sense of what healthy food was. I never knew what I should or shouldn't eat. I had done so many different diets that completely contradicted each other, so I didn't know what the right information was.

Junior year was a culmination of my eating disorder; I didn't want to eat because of the fear I have about gaining weight, I didn't know what to eat because of the confusion from diets, and I couldn't eat because I was so depressed that I had no appetite. I went through multiple waves of not eating which caused me to lose so much weight that I fit back into my clothes from middle school. I'm at a point now where I'm still struggling with disordered eating and negative body image. It's so easy to slip back into that mindset, and I've noticed it comes in waves. A lot of it stems from shame around being different from the standards that have been presented to me. There are times where I notice my thighs completely touch and the fascination of a thigh gap will pop back up. I'm trying to unlearn the ideas of beauty that have been ingrained in my head, but it's not easy. Even though I'm not around nearly as many skinny, white girls as I used to be, I'm still being affected by the mentality that was formed when I was young.

Feeling different than the students around them impacts students of color in a variety of ways. It impacts our academic performance, and more importantly our self-esteem, self-efficacy, and overall mental health which contributes to the impact on academics. I personally have experiences with different impacts and how they have evolved and created lasting effects in my life. Academically speaking, feeling different can make students of color doubt our place in a room, and doubt the abilities that we have. Often, we feel less competent and intelligent than the white students in the room. Every student has a unique experience, but in general, black and brown students feel less intelligent, while Asian students are stereotyped as smart which has a different negative effect.

When I look around the classroom and see that I'm the only student of color there, it's common for me to not try as hard because the possibility of succeeding seems slim. Even in elementary school, I could sense that honors classes were not meant to be a space for me. I felt like an interloper, even if I didn't have the language to express it. There was a lot that I had to bottle up because my white peers did not understand. I never could fit in with my program without being embarrassed of who I was, and I was kept away from the other program entirely. I am grateful for the privilege that allowed me to be in the honors program, but I believe it did more harm for me than good. I've always wondered how different my life would be if I'd been in general instead.

The lack of black students in the room makes advanced classes a white space for white students to succeed while students of color are pushed to the sides and forced to make the best of their situation. The environment in these classes is already competitive because of the rigor of the curriculum, and knowing that no one is in the same position as me makes showing up and working hard a difficult task. The class for me that I experienced this into the fullest extent was AP chemistry my sophomore year. I'll be using this class as an example of many issues because it perfectly illustrates the inequity I'm describing, but I'll now focus in on how feeling different than the other students made a huge impact on my experience, and was one of the reasons why that class felt like a lost cause for me.

> *"I feel uncomfortable in every honors class because it's a whole bunch of white people and I'm the lone big, black man in there. I don't relate to nobody and they're just different, like personality wise. They have different experiences, and they have different advantages; I don't relate to them at all."*

> *"Since first grade I've been on the honors track, it's dominated by mostly white and Asian kids, so being Asian I fit in for the most part. But, most of the Asian kids weren't Filipino, they were lighter, Vietnamese or Chinese, so it was hard to find my place."*

Freshman year, when I was signing up for my classes, I was aware that AP classes at my school were white and East Asian dominated. I had never been in one, so I didn't know exactly how extreme it would be, and I hoped it wouldn't be as bad as the honors program in elementary and middle school. I loved chemistry the year before, so signing up for AP chemistry seemed like an obvious choice. At my school, first year chemistry classes were mixed with honors students and regular students because the same course was taught with only a few differences in the content between the two. So, the class was diverse: different grades, different races, different reasons for being there. I credit part of my success in that class to its diversity and my teacher who knew how to meet everyone's individual needs.

I guess part of me hoped, despite my knowledge of the reality, that my AP class would have a similar atmosphere to my first-year class. I knew I was wrong from the second I walked in. No one else in the room was black, so I knew they have didn't experiences like I did, or have an understanding of my position. And I could tell that from the start. I knew who many of these students were, I'd been in classes with them since elementary school, but now they treated me like a stranger. In one word, the atmosphere was cold. Within one class period, I could feel all my personality, all my blackness, all of me, was being sucked up slowly.

I could've told anyone from the first day that I was not going to do well in the class. I would give it a shot, I wanted to prove them and myself wrong, but seeing that no other black student elected to be in that class terrified me. I showed up every day to walk out feeling like a shell of myself after enduring the snickers when I asked for clarification, the eye rolls when I offered an answer, and the condescending looks in everyone's eyes. I already knew I didn't belong there, and my classmates sure did a good job at reminding me. I felt like how I used to feel in elementary school, always needing people to see me for the intelligent person that I am. This time though, I started to feel like maybe I was as dumb as they assumed me to be. AP chemistry is a hard class, and when I felt like I couldn't ask a question without getting bashed, I stopped asking them, and stopped understanding the content. I didn't feel comfortable asking anyone in the room for help. When I did ask to see someone's answers to check mine with, I would be accused of trying to copy them. My classmates continued to turn their backs on me throughout the course because I was different from them.

> *"In middle school, I had friends who were in my honors Language Arts class who took honors math while I wasn't in the honors math program. They were almost all white kids, so it made it seem like I couldn't be in the honors math program or succeed in the honors program in general. I thought I had to dumb myself down as a person of color. I was never told it was ok to be smart. In high school I realized that it's ok to be smart, succeed, and show them what I can do."*

I took measures for most of my years in school to stand out as little as possible through my overall presentation. Throughout middle school and into the first years of high school, I always felt the need to look my best, so there would be less to judge about my appearance. In sixth grade I was convinced that I was not allowed to repeat an outfit because people would judge me. In class, I would only answer questions if I was sure that I was right. I might have known I was smart, but the other kids in my class didn't always see me that way unless I shoved it down their throats. I needed to be accepted by these people because I was terrified of being laughed at, being unpopular, or people thinking I was dumb. I was hyper aware of myself and everything that I did.

The social aspect of school is challenging when students feel different. Students of color in white dominated classes generally have two choices: assimilate and have friends, or stand out as themselves and risk being alone. Not every student of color has the same experiences feeling different in white classrooms, and not everyone reacts to it in the same way. For most of my life, I chose to assimilate with the white crowd in order to have them as my friends. Where I'm at now, I take pride in my clear differences, and do the opposite of what I did before by accentuating them, and making it clear to people that I will not take any shit from them. Looking back, my white friendships that I had during my years of assimilation weren't genuine and stemmed from a place of self-hatred and self-doubt. The friends I have now take me for who I am, and make me feel appreciated.

"Being in an all-black school when I was in elementary school, it didn't feel like anything. It felt like I was accepted, there weren't any differences that set me apart from other people. Kids didn't have a reason, except just not liking me, to not talk or interact with me. The transition to a majority white private school was confusing. I didn't really notice anything racial in my elementary school, which was all black, so when I entered middle school, I didn't understand what set me apart. I didn't realize why

people weren't talking to me, why people looked at me weird, why my hair was so interesting to people. I had a conversation with my mom, and I realized that I was different because of the way I looked."

In eighth grade, I had finally found a friend group. After my shitty time with having no friends in seventh grade, I was beyond excited to be included again. It was a group of white girls who were considered popular in my grade. I genuinely enjoyed being friends with them, and had a lot of love for them, but choosing to be in that friend group came from the need to be accepted by white people. I felt like I needed a friend group to have a solid social standing when I went into high school, and I wanted to fit in the way that they did.

I was sexually assaulted for the first time that year. The guy who raped me was within that same friend group. He was liked by all of them and popular overall. I remember thinking he was sweet and funny when I first met him. We talked during class, and I considered him a friend. I trusted him. It was middle school, so only a week after I met him I quickly started hearing from other people that he liked me. I didn't feel the same about him, but didn't want to reject him right away because he was close friends with my friends, so that could cause tension. We hung out a couple of times, and it was fine. He kissed me, but I told him I wasn't interested. He didn't like that answer.

After he raped me, I didn't know what to do. I didn't know who to tell, or who to trust. I wanted to report it, but I was terrified of doing that because I didn't think anyone would believe me. During this time, I was struggling with depression and suicidal actions which put me in the hospital twice. I thought people would use my mental health against me, and I would be labeled as crazy. He went ahead and told everyone for me, describing it as consensual sex which it was not. The girls who I was friends with laughed at it, and brushed it off when I explained that I hadn't wanted to have sex with him. Even after explaining in detail that I was raped, I was pressured by him and others to continue being sexual and romantic with him to make it seem like I was into him. It disgusted me, but I had no idea how to get out of it. I had to see him every day at school, and he was always wanting me to come over to his house where he would torment me even by shooting me with an airsoft gun unless I agreed to have sex. There was a time where he hid my phone, wouldn't allow me to leave his house, and repeatedly shot me with an airsoft gun because I kissed another guy. I felt like I had no control over my body or my actions because of the power he held over me and that there was no one on my side.

The friend group that I was in was completely aware of what had happened. They knew that I was raped and abused by this guy. Still, they acted like nothing had ever happened. I had to endure countless parties, lunches, football games being around him, hearing his voice, and seeing how everyone else was fine with him being there. I felt forced to put on a smile around him, and pretend it never happened. Even though on the outside I held myself together, inside I was screaming. I should've left; I was putting myself through so much by not, but I couldn't do it. Why did I feel such a strong need to be friends with these white girls even though they kept me in proximity to my rapist? Why didn't I value myself more? Why didn't I stand up for myself earlier? I feared coming to terms with it and acknowledging my pain. I feared not being accepted by other people. Despite all my fear around fighting for myself, I couldn't bottle it up forever. Being around him made my skin crawl, and I eventually began to associate my friends directly with him which made me resent them. It took me months into freshman year to say something.

My years of feeling different from white kids and my internalized self-doubt made it difficult for me to leave that toxic friend group. My standing in the friend group always felt unstable because I was different from them, and at first, I didn't want to take chances by saying something. I needed to retain their acceptance because I had been hurt and scarred from rejection over the years. Even after I made my exit out of the group, I questioned my choice and whether I would ever find friends again. I felt like there was nowhere I would ever fit in and be valued. I've never healed from this incident. Thinking about it now, all the feelings of shame, misery, and disgust I felt back then are coming up to the surface. I learned a lot from that pain; I would rather have those white girls dislike me than have them as "friends" and be violated by having my rapist in my life.

"When I was in fifth grade, someone said, 'Your eyes are so far apart.' It made me extremely self-conscious and insecure. So, what I did for the next three years, I kept my glasses on and never took them off, even when I was playing sports and they would break. Now I'm okay with my eyes, because I've accepted who I am, but it really got to me."

Students of color have wounds that aren't addressed. Many of us have spent years comparing ourselves to our white peers which only accentuates the physical and cultural differences we have. With where I'm at now, I can see that the differences which clearly do exist should be appreciated. It's beautiful that we have differences. However, with where our society is, those differences are looked down on. They're stigmatized and weaponized against students of color. Because of this, it's common for black and brown students to minimize their features, both physical and cultural, to make it easier for them to get through their school days. One thing that I did to cope with feeling different was I accentuated the "white" parts of myself. This included appearing as non-black as possible, being smart, having white friends and focusing only on having a relationship with my mom because my dad is black. I would only wear brands that I associated with whiteness. I straightened my hair a lot or wore it in buns. I only would hang out with people also in the honors program in order to fit in. Coping in this way didn't allow me to explore myself without the fear of judgement.

"I'm a freshman so I'm transitioning into high school, but going to a majority people of color school after being around only white people for so long is hard. All middle school I found that my main goal was to not be a stereotype or a monolith, I wanted to be an individual. I didn't want people to look at me and assume I was like every other black person. Coming to high school I was going to continue the same thing.

I realized that to fit in with the people of color you had to act a certain way, wear your hair a certain way and do all these things I wasn't aware you had to do. I worked so hard in middle school to fit in with people who didn't look like me, that it's hard to reconnect with people who look like me."

Years of forced assimilation leaves students of color disconnected from their peers of color once they have them. There were a few times in middle school where I had opportunities to get to know the other black kids at my school, but I was worried that I would be "too white" for them since I had been surrounding myself with white people for so long. I let these opportunities go because of fear of the unknown, fear of rejection, and fear of judgment. Those long years had stunted my growth in connecting with my black identity and other people with the same identity.

In high school, after I ditched my white girl friend group, I noticed a sharp change in the way I was treated in majority white classrooms. When I started distancing myself away from whiteness, I started receiving more micro aggressions, and the sense that they weren't comfortable with me being there. I had been in classes with some of these kids since first grade, and had been known as the one black girl who was in honors classes. They hadn't treated me the same as each other, but they at least recognized my place in the room. Instantly when I noticed the shift, a lot of anger and resentment came up. Instead of going back to what I used to do, assimilating and making them accept me, I hyper exaggerated the fact that I was black. I played the stereotypical part of the loud and angry black girl because I knew that I would be seen that way anyway. I wasn't going to let them erase my blackness like they had done for so many years.

Feeling different shouldn't be bad. Differences should be acknowledged without exploiting or demeaning them. Colorblindness shouldn't be the goal because it erases what makes us unique. It's no secret that different races and ethnicities have physical and cultural differences. We are all able to learn from each other in some way, and students of color contribute so much if we feel comfortable expressing it. When whiteness is seen as the norm, it becomes an impossible standard that people of color are pressured by society to reach. Instead of loving who I am, I spent years of my life trying to be white. It did more than manifest self hate, it made me feel like I needed to be accepted by white people to have any worth, so my actions prioritized that. In and out of school, I never felt comfortable expressing myself as a black person, sharing my experiences, or challenging white people until I was a sophomore in high school. I hope the differences students of color have can be seen as a positive, to the schools, teachers, and most importantly, ourselves.

Struggles

I decided to take AP chemistry my sophomore year even though people warned me that it was a hard class because I was good at chemistry the year before. I was excited about it, and was even thinking about majoring in chemistry in college. Even with the confidence and excitement I had, I knew that AP classes weren't made for me. As much as I dreaded that aspect, I wanted to believe that I would be able to create a space for myself in that class that would allow me to succeed. I wanted to make a statement to white students and AP teachers that I was there to stay, I was capable, and black students are just as intelligent as white and Asian students, and we deserved to be in AP classes too. I knew it would be a challenge because of the advanced level content, the adversities that come with being in a white space, and my mental health likely getting in the way. It was going to take a lot of perseverance and determination to make it through.

During the first quarter, I did all the assigned homework, asked for help if I was confused and studied hard for my first tests.

It wasn't easy, but I managed to end the quarter with a B grade, and I was proud of myself. Quickly into second quarter, the class took a turn for the worse. The content started moving faster and faster, and I fell behind. I soon realized that AP chemistry was a lot different from the first year; the content was far more in depth, the other students were more competitive, and the teacher was less supportive. Meanwhile stress in my personal life was accumulating, making it difficult for me to focus. I was failing at balancing school with caring for my mental health. I knew I needed help in the class, but when I asked other students for help, they either responded condescendingly or became annoyed. That's when I stopped asking for help, and isolated myself from the other students in the class. I refused to raise my hand in class when the teacher asked for questions because if I got the answer wrong, I heard snickers.

I went to my teacher at first for help, but as there was more and more I didn't understand, it felt like a lost cause to try. I felt uncomfortable disclosing to him the things I was going through that made it more difficult for me to focus, so I made up other excuses that he didn't accept. I was stranded, alone, in a class that had been built for me to fail. As my grade dropped, it weighed me down and made me feel like a failure, and I started to associate the class with feelings of shame and inferiority. I stopped caring about the class all together because of how shitty it made me feel about myself; I only put in the bare minimum effort needed to pass. My motivation to do well in chemistry, a subject that I had previously loved, slipped away by the end of the first semester. There was no point trying in a class that wasn't meant for me to succeed in than it was for the other students who had found support within each other. At first I blamed it on myself, but realized it wasn't about my intelligence or capabilities. It seemed that everyone else had access to the resources needed to succeed and felt comfortable in the class except for me.

The year went on and we were approaching the big AP chemistry test. I honestly have no explanation why I wasted one hundred and two dollars of my mom's money to take a test on a subject I didn't know a damn thing about. Seriously, I couldn't tell you one thing we learned that year. However, my misguided self was convinced I could take that test, and potentially not fail. The night before the test, I decided to do a little reviewing, and I promptly gave up because absolutely nothing I read in the textbook rang a bell, and successfully teaching myself a year's worth of material in one night was unlikely. I woke up the next morning at the ungodly time of six in order to take the exam. The first thing I noticed was that everyone was white or Asian. I was one of five black students taking the test which meant that from all the AP chemistry classes at my school, only five black students were included. The test began, and I have never felt dumber and more ashamed in my academic career than I did during the multiple hours of testing. My ears rang the whole time, and nausea consumed me. I couldn't answer a single question with any confidence. I sat in silence, doing nothing for hours because I ran out of guesses before the time limit was up. If I had to describe academic failure, this was it.

After the test, I was mad. I spent a lot of my time ranting to people about my experience in the class. Anyone who listened would learn that I was against everything to do with chemistry and the AP system. I got my score back, and unsurprisingly received a 1. I remember my mom congratulating me on not getting a 0 before

I explained that there is no 0, and 1 is the lowest possible score. I scratched out the idea of majoring in the subject; I decided it wasn't for me, essentially gave up on chemistry all together, and vowed to never take another AP science class again. Not only because the subject was challenging, but because being in an all-white environment where I felt like I was little to nothing was not worth putting an AP science on my transcript. I passed the class with a C and moved on.

Academics aren't meant to be easy by any means. School should challenge us, and overall give us the knowledge that will prepare us for the future. It's supposed to be simple, try hard in school, get good grades, go to college and have a job to support yourself. Growing up, I truly believed that straight A's were a given if students showed up and tried their best. By the end up sixth grade, I learned that it wasn't that easy, and getting an A was harder for me than others. I know very few people who can say that they've never had a hard time in school, but of those people, most of them are white. And even of the people who have had struggles in school, students of color overall have had a harder time succeeding.

Even though it is easier for some people to explain this by saying that students of color are lazy, entitled, or not as smart, there are real reasons that factor into why students of color tend to struggle more academically than white students. As much as some people like to ignore this and act like it's not a problem, it is, and we can't ignore it anymore. When so many students of color are failing and dropping out, it's clear that we can't blame it on the individual students; this is a systemic issue. I want to make a clear distinction: the concept of having an educated society has good intent, however the system in place is not structured for everyone to have the same chance. Education, as a concept, is well intended, but the institution, like all American institutions, is racist. The systems in place cater academics towards white people while the other groups fight against the odds to succeed. Some reasons that students of color struggle in academics include; excessive societal and family pressure, lack of support, being in an uncomfortable environment and lack of motivation after years of working twice as hard to come only half as far.

I view the way students of color struggle in school as a cycle. It starts with the challenge that school is meant to have, then the adversities that come with being a person of color in America are added. On top of that, we often are dealing with other things in our personal lives. We start to struggle, and our grades slip. Teachers then assume we are doing poorly because we're lazy and irresponsible, not because something bigger is impacting us. They don't reach out to give us support because of these assumptions, so unless we advocate for ourselves, we continue to struggle. The cycle continues unless someone intervenes.

> *"In high school taking AP classes that are mostly white, I still feel so unmotivated. It's beyond belief. It's not even just about the class environment anymore, it's just about the realization of how deep racist systems and the hopelessness of succeeding. I'm thriving outside of school, I'm part of many organizing communities. Inside of school, I feel like I can't do anything because it's not made for me. Being Asian, the system is built for me, but being brown, it isn't and that's a weird dynamic. I'm at the point right now where I don't even get stressed about school because I don't even care."*

My mom often jokes that third grade was my academic peak, and I agree. I don't interpret it as being the year I was most intelligent because I really hope I'm at least a little smarter than my eight-year-old self. I see it as the year I had the most motivation for school, the year I tried the hardest, cared the most, and believed in myself. From then on, my interest and motivation in school has diminished. Flash forward to high school, I have refined my method of putting the least amount of energy into school while still managing a reasonable GPA. This method worked better for some classes than others. I remember the moment that I realized that I was meant to fail my AP chemistry class; not the moment my grade dropped below passing, but the moment I understood the underlying system impacting my success. I didn't have the same resources as the other students, I wasn't given the same respect and I didn't have the same support. Of course, this doesn't necessarily mean that every black student is going to fail AP chemistry, but the odds certainly aren't in our favor. Once we realize that this isn't all in on us, or made up in our heads, we must figure out where we want to go from there. It's not a clear choice. Giving up, dropping the class, putting in minimal effort is easy, but it can feel like we're letting the system win. Pushing through doesn't mean things get any easier, but maybe the only way to eventually make a change is to first get through it.

"Middle school was the time I started to connect with myself in terms of South-East Asian identity and being Filipino. Being in the all-white environment, I was sick all the time, I didn't go to class, it took a toll on my body and my grades. That was the time when my grades were ass and being in this all white environment I didn't want

*to show up, I didn't want to put effort
into it, I didn't have a lot of motivation."*

Academic struggles lead to and are then impacted poor health, physical and mental. Education becomes harmful when it is put above mental health. Every student should be aware that they're allowed to take care of themselves even if it negatively impacts their performance in school. Unfortunately, it isn't made clear that mental health should be prioritized over school. When education is hurting students of color without benefiting them, there's clearly an issue. Even public education isn't free when it's taking a tax on your mind and body. Often, this will eventually end up with the student continuing to spiral unless someone steps in to help.

One of years I struggled most regarding tending to my mental health while staying on top of school was in eighth grade. The struggle I was going through during this time was bigger than school. I couldn't do well in school because of it, but the problem wasn't rooted in school itself, and it was out of my control. The winter of that year was a dark time for me, and I consider it a major turning point in my life. It started with two suicide attempts at the beginning of December in response to cyber bullying which put me in the hospital and forced me to miss a few weeks of school. Something inside me broke during this period; I lost the childhood innocence that I used to have, and started to see myself as a monster. I started self-destructing through cutting myself, lashing out, refusing help, and pushing people away. School seemed minimal to me compared to everything else I was going through, so it dropped far down on my list of priorities. Getting out of bed in the morning became impossible. I continued missing school because I was too depressed to move. I wanted to die, so things like passing my classes seemed pointless.

I was already struggling, and everything became worse after I was raped. Going to school after the assault became torture; he was in one of my classes and I hated being near him because I had to mask my feelings while he would talk to me, touch me, and make me beyond uncomfortable. I started to associate school with seeing him, and dreaded going every day. It was impossible for me to focus on my work when my mind was far away from that. My grades took a hit, and my teachers started to notice. They seemed fed up with my behavior; I don't think they knew what to do with me. I was barely coming to class, never knew what was going on, and always asked to go to the nurse to lie down. People of any race struggle with mental health issues that can impact their academics, but I think that the way my teachers responded to it would've been different if I was white. It was easier for them to lump me into the stereotypical category of bad black kids instead of taking time to check in with me. I wasn't given the benefit of the doubt, and it wasn't until my white mother intervened that they started to take my issues seriously.

"At the beginning of this school year, I started taking four APs. AP chem, AP World, AP Calculus, and AP Japanese. That was a big leap from the previous year when I was taking zero. I wish someone had told me about how hard it would be, even my counselor didn't say shit about it. The first three weeks of school I was mentally breaking

down every single day. I felt like I was high all the time because I was just so out of touch with reality. I would cry, I would find myself just wandering at night and I just wondering how the fuck I got there. I felt so dehumanized and I felt like I had nobody to talk to. There aren't many support systems for people of color at school and being Asian I felt like I couldn't ask for the help I needed. If my mom and dad didn't notice how hard school was on me and how much pressure I put on myself and how stressed out I was, I really think I would've just dropped dead at some point, that's how bad it was."

Eighth grade might have been the start of my mental health issues impacting school, but as life continued, it worsened and progressed in high school. By the end of third quarter of sophomore year, I was skipping at least three classes a day and seriously falling behind. Only one of my teachers bothered to ask me what was going on. At the time it seemed like none of them really cared whether I did well; I was not their problem. I was more than happy that they let me leave class whenever I wanted without questioning it, but looking back, it's disappointing. A lot of the times I stepped out of class I went to the bathroom to cry on the floor, or went home to try to kill myself. In order to get through the year, I had to get a 504 plan with my school counselor. The 504 plan basically said I was depressed enough for it to be a valid reason for my poor performance. I was given accommodations like being able to turn assignments in a few days late, leaving class to take short breaks, and taking tests alone. The plan honestly did not do much to help me succeed, but I was lucky enough to get it, and in a short period of time, which is not the case for everyone. My teachers hadn't checked on me when I ran out of class crying multiple times, but when they were informed I had a 504, they all individually pulled me aside to talk. The unfortunate realization I made was that my teachers probably assumed I was being delinquent and that was why they did not check in on me. I was a good student before my depression and anxiety were debilitating, so I don't see why they would assume that except for the fact that I am a black student. Teachers should be doing more to check in with their students, including students of color, and not assume that they are being lazy and are a lost cause.

Along with the other adversities we face, students of color are pressured by our communities, our families and society to have high achievements. When we don't, it feels like it's our fault for not living up to expectations. We so desperately want to prove society wrong that we pack the burden onto our own shoulders. During times that I've struggled academically for whatever reason, a lot of shame around letting people down comes up. I personally don't receive a ton of pressure from my family, but I do feel pressured by society to not let the statistics about black students be true for me. That's why I challenge myself even though I'm aware I'm not supposed to succeed in advanced classes; I feel the need to be an outlier, and to show other black students that they can be too. It's easier said than done because there's a structural reason why black students overall struggle in school.

"I've always been good at math, but even

though I am capable, and I am comfortable with the subject, there are times when I struggle. Everyone struggles, nobody's fucking perfect. Whenever I struggled I always felt so alone and I felt like I couldn't ask anyone for help. I couldn't reach out to anyone. Especially because of the stereotype that Asians are smart, I felt like I couldn't disgrace my race and never asked a question in class. It was getting better last year, and I was participating in class. Lately in AP classes I felt the same way, like I couldn't raise my hand and ask a fucking question."

When a student of color walks into a classroom of only other white students, they immediately become the representative for their entire race or ethnicity which comes from the societal idea that all nonwhite people are the same as everyone else in their same race or ethnic group. Imagine being expected to carry all that weight every day. It often feels like if we make a mistake, it will be reflected onto everyone else who looks like us. Therefore, it can feel like we are not allowed to make mistakes, ask for help, or anything else that might cause people to look down on not just us, but everyone from our background. White students can have more individualism, without their actions being generalized to the actions of all white students. For Asian students, the stereotype is that they are smart, and especially that they are good at math. This stereotype puts greater pressure on Asian students to be smart, or they will be judged by their peers for not being what they are assumed to be. In middle school, I heard people in my class making fun of an Asian student who didn't know how to do a math problem and said, "If they can't do math, what are they good for?"

> *"I don't have a strong support system at school. I find most of my support at home from my family. I go to the teachers that I have a strong relationship with, regardless of the subject when I need help."*

> *"The teachers are mostly white; I think sometimes they don't do everything that they could be doing. I don't feel like I have a strong support system at my school. The teachers like to say that they're there for you, but honestly the teachers don't try hard enough. Some do, but in my opinion the majority don't. I go to my extracurriculars to ask for academic help."*

Though there are programs at some schools dedicated to supporting students of color, they are not always accessible to all students or available at every school. Having support in school is crucial for success. Personally, I do not have a specific support system at school. Sometimes I'm lucky enough to have a teacher who is supportive, and I can go to for help, but that is usually not the case. I want to suggest that teachers to put a box in their classroom that students can leave notes about issues they are having, in the class or in their personal life because it's hard to initiate a conversation with a teacher, and leaving them a note feels less stressful. An easy way of doing this is having every student answer the question, "Do you need a check in?" once a week, and put their answer in the box. All students deserve the benefit of the doubt when they are struggling, and when teachers let their bias dictate who they support, they're letting down black and brown students. I want all students of color to feel like success is achievable in any level of class. Feeling challenged is good, but feeling like our efforts are futile and the outcome is out of our control means something isn't working, and it needs to be improved.

Representation

I started questioning my gender and sexuality when I was fourteen, in eighth grade, and it was a difficult transitional period for me because I didn't have any resources to guide my exploration. I knew about gay people growing up; I had many gay family friends and thought nothing of it. I wasn't fully aware of transgender people until middle school, and I'm pretty sure it was because of Caitlyn Jenner. Other than limited information from the media, I didn't have much information on what it meant to be queer.

I came out publicly when I was fourteen as bisexual. It went fine, most people around me couldn't have cared less. Still, I didn't have any information on what my identity meant, how I could explore it, and how it would impact my life. I didn't know who to go to with questions, or how to find more people who felt the same way. Teachers never spoke on the queer community, even in health class where it should have been brought up. As far as I knew, I had an identity that I didn't really understand, people around me didn't want to talk about, and wasn't an important part of me. Later that year, when I started to question my gender, I had a similar feeling of confusion and lack of representation. I had nothing to guide me through this self-exploration.

In the spring, after I had come out as bisexual, and when I was digging into my gender, was also when I was raped for the first time. The assault took away a lot from me; in simpler terms, it fucked me up. I felt like an object after it happened, and felt that I was going to be used by men the way they wanted to use me. There was no room there for me to decide what I wanted to identify as, or who I wanted to be attracted to. What I went through broke a piece of me, and I didn't go back to fix it for years. I stopped exploring who I was and conformed to who I thought men wanted me to be. The next few years, I presented as a cisgender, heterosexual girl who dated cisgender boys and allowed them to walk all over me.

After I had told my boyfriend freshman year that I was bisexual, and he reacted horribly, I decided to be straight. Sexuality isn't a choice though. As much as I tried to tell myself that I was straight, I couldn't fully erase that part of myself. Being in a monogamous, heterosexual relationship allowed me to mask my queerness, but it never was gone. It wasn't until junior year when I decided to confront my sexuality again. Once I got out of that relationship and didn't have to hide it anymore, sexuality wasn't a huge question for me; I knew I was attracted to all types of people.

Unfortunately, history repeated itself. Beginning of junior year, when I was genuinely doing well for the first time in months and trying to figure out who I was, I got raped for the second time. It's hard to express the amount of damage this incident did to me. I didn't want to look at myself for weeks. I spiraled into a long self-harm relapse. I lost trust in myself, with men, and with my friends who were there that night. I constantly felt a sense of impending doom, like there was nothing I could do to keep this from happening to me. For the second time, I felt like all my control was gone. What was the point of trying to find who I was when these boys continued to take everything away from me for their own desires? I fell back into habit and got into a relationship with a cisgender boy and tried to be who he wanted me to be. In some ways, being in a relationship made me feel less at risk for sexual assault, but it also put me in a position where I felt pressured to have sex that I didn't want to have. Our relationship ended abruptly during the winter of junior year when I was raped again, for the third time, and blamed for cheating. My now ex-boyfriend, who I would have hoped to support me through this traumatic event, villainized me and put me through even more pain which nailed it in my head that cisgender men were not safe, and I could not trust them.

I realized that I wasn't in these relationships because I wanted to be, but because I felt like I had to be. The trauma that I had accumulated throughout these past few years had broken me, but I wasn't going to let fear and past experiences prevent me from figuring out who I could be if it was my choice. I spent time thinking through my behavior, my appearance, my identity to see if it was based around my desires or the desires of the men who had abused me. The pretty, feminine, straight, cisgender girl was who they wanted me to be; it was how they could hold power over me. I knew that it was appealing to them, but looking in the mirror, the only positive thoughts I had about myself were about how I would be perceived by them. I didn't like how I looked. It didn't feel authentic to me. I was so much more than the box that I had kept myself in for years. Even though it does for other people, identifying as a cisgender girl didn't provide that freedom for me. I could now see with extreme clarity that being transgender was an identity I held. Figuring out that the true version of myself was genderqueer and transmasculine took many years, a lot of detours, and facing the impact of my trauma. I'm still working on gaining complete control over my life through therapy, and it will take time.

I'm proud of where I've gotten myself despite all the challenges, and my persistence to live my life the way I want to. Through this journey I've learned about myself, as well as the lack of resources and education provided to me. People of all races can be sexuaul assalt victims or queer, but as a person who is also black, my experience with both is different because of the way my race interacts with all other aspects of my identity. There was nowhere clear for me to go for help after I was raped, and there was nowhere for me to talk to someone about my sexuality or gender. I wasn't taught anything in school about my rights after being assaulted, or about how to explore my different identities. The lack of support and representation I had in school made this journey longer and more difficult for me, contributing to the adversities I was already facing.

Representation is a vital component in a well-rounded, accurate education that works for all students. White people, white history, and white culture is well represented, and so are other mainstream cultures. Other groups of people are left out in different aspects of education. I've found that this lack of representation within education is prevalent in three main areas: the content taught, the people teaching, and the people making decisions for the school. Representation in these areas is important for all students to be served equally and to be given education that covers a wide range of perspectives and groups of people. Representation is also lacking within resources at schools; many marginalized groups don't have information or other necessary resources provided for them at school.

"My native culture is important to me and a big part of who I am. Every year in school, in history class specifically, there's a day or two set aside where we talk about Native American people and the culture. It's happened every year I can remember. It's the same talk every time, usually about how they're represented in the media or about stereotypes. It's important to realize there's a lot more to native people and native culture than stereotypes. The rest of the year native people are sort of forgotten about. Unfortunately, I've noticed this happen with a lot of nonwhite history."

"The most representation I've had is learning about the Harlem renaissance and slavery.

There is nothing about the inventions and achievements of black people. What we learn about the history of black culture and the US. history of slaves is warped sometimes. A lot of my history teachers had said there was already similar systems of slavery in Africa. So, when white people took slaves from Africa, the system was already occurring, and it was just bringing slavery to America. This was not accurate at all."

Schools teach selective pieces of history that they want us to learn, rather than the big picture and the overall reality. It continues to uphold white supremacy in American society; it is leaving out the history of marginalized groups because they are viewed as inferior, and telling history in a way that favors white people. Furthermore, we don't learn about certain history because it would be beneficial for the people who have power for us to forget about, so parts of United States history that make the country look bad are watered down or skewed. The Japanese internment camps were barely touched on in my history education, and the genocide of native Americans was smoothed over to seem less horrific. I think that we should be learning from and acknowledging our ugly past rather than ignoring it to have it repeat itself, but there's a lot of history we don't learn unless we pursue an education of it later.

History classes tend to be the most Eurocentric classes. They can teach students about history from all cultures and places, but almost always focus on Europe and the only time the history of other continents comes up is when Europe was colonizing them.

It's almost as if the history of other places is negligible up until Europe contacts them. Because white people have caused nothing but destruction to the places they colonize, the history that we learn about ourselves is depressing. We don't get to learn about the greatness of our ancestors because it's overshadowed by how white people took it all away. Moving through the education system as a black student was difficult in this aspect. I was taught all the names and backgrounds of European colonizers, but didn't know anything about my own history. This impacted me growing up especially because of my mixed-race background. Living with my white mom, I didn't get much exposure to black culture as a child. I felt a deep disconnect from black culture at a young age since I didn't have have black culture in my home life, and school didn't teach me anything about black history besides slavery, so I struggled for most of my life with figuring out what it meant for me to be black.

> *"Queer black folks have taught me everything. It's not their job, but I learned so much about leadership from them. The education that I see as important comes from outside of school. I'm lucky for the education I've received, but what's valuable to me has come from outside the American education system."*

Attending school for over a decade hasn't taught me much that I actually take outside of the classroom and use. Some of the basic stuff content has been useful, like knowing how to convey my ideas through writing, but it's been four years since I had to memorize all the countries in Europe, and I have yet to find a use for that. The skills I've learned are how to cram information for a test, how to write an essay in one night, and how to bullshit my way through class work. I can do my best in a class, get good grades, and leave the quarter feeling as if I have no greater knowledge on the subject. It feels like going to school has become a formality for me, not an opportunity for learning, which is disappointing. Education is supposed to be enriching, and though I'm grateful for having the opportunity to be in school I feel as if it's not providing me a good education.

The people who I look to learn from are my community leaders, mentors, and activists, not my teachers. From them I've developed my leadership, my facilitation skills, and public speaking. My views on racism and society have been developed completely outside of my academic education. Part of this is because what I learn in school doesn't seem like it's meant for me. The lack of representation of people like me makes it hard to be interested in what I'm learning. I've always been aware of that, but after attending an event called Freedom School, I saw with more clarity how much the education system chooses not to teach us. The Tyree Scott Freedom School was brought to my attention by my friend in AP chemistry. We were the only students of color in the class, so of course we stuck together. I remember one day I was looking over and they were working on something that caught my eye. When I asked what it was, they explained to me that they were doing work for Youth Undoing Institutionalized Racism (YUIR) which was where they organized. Immediately I was interested; I'd been trying to find more ways to get into organizing and learning from those communities. I asked how I could check it out, and they said to come to Freedom School.

For the next few weeks, I was awaiting this event. My friend hadn't told me much about it except for that it was led by queer black people and we would be talking about racism. I didn't know what to expect, but was very excited to fill my brain with whatever I would learn. When I walked into the space for the first time, I felt like I was walking into open arms. Everyone was welcoming, kind, and most importantly for me, people of color. In school I'm lectured by a white man about my history, but here I was brought into the space by a group of young, queer, people of color who wanted me to be there, and wanted me to learn. They spoke not only from their knowledge, but also from their personal experiences. I learned more during the four days of Freedom School than I have in any full course. I learned things that have stuck in my brain, and that have been consistently useful for me. A lot of the racial analysis in this book has stemmed from what I learned in there. I felt more confident in talking about race and racism, and defending my arguments by going to that event. I urge everyone to attend a Freedom School, it changed my life.

"The history teachers at my school make their own curriculum, we don't learn out of a textbook. They use their own articles and assignments which touch on racism and social issues. The first thing my history teacher said to me freshman year was, 'We don't learn out of a textbook. If someone asks, we do, but we don't.'"

The standard American education curriculum doesn't incorporate critical topics in society, such as race, gender, current issues, and more topics that should be widely spoken about in school. Teachers have a difficult role to play; balancing what they are required to cover with what they should incorporate. A lot of times I've noticed teachers skip over a perfect opportunity to discuss race. When I ask them why, it's usually because they're uncomfortable with the topic and don't know how to go about teaching it. I appreciate when teachers acknowledge the holes they have in their knowledge, but it still isn't an excuse to let ignorance on race continue because they haven't taken the time to educate themselves. Teachers should be required to be competent in facilitating important discussions and have background knowledge on racism in order to give students a complete education.

"This year I had my first black teacher ever. It completely changed my drive to succeed in my class. She's a teacher who I can relate to at a level that's deeper than school. She understands that I got through things that white students don't and she supports me. I would like to see more representation in faculty. Teachers of color are important for student's color to be able to build relationships."

"I've had one teacher of color, for ethnic studies. The teacher has their own personal experiences to add into the curriculum. With white teachers, you have to say the academic thing when talking about race, but with

teachers of color you can talk about your own experiences. The curriculum is more catered towards you and you feel represented."

We need more black teachers. If I had the power to change one thing about schools to create the most positive change, I would hire a bunch of black teachers at every single school. Representation for students of color needs to be seen in the people teaching them. It wouldn't fix everything, of course, but I have confidence that many of the problems at schools could be minimized with more black teachers present. It might take a while for it to start dismantling the institutionalized racism at schools because that reflects American society overall, but I know that it would instantly create many positive impacts at schools. The few times that I've had a teacher of color, I was able to relax and feel more comfortable in a class. The presence of a teacher of color makes me feel welcome in the class even if I'm one of the few black students. Not all people of color have the same experiences, but there's a certain level of understanding that most of us have with one another. We go through things and have experiences that white people struggle understanding. A problem that comes with hiring teachers of color is keeping them there. Just last year at my school, a bunch of young teachers of color were hired, and now only a year later, they've been displaced. Whether they leave because they don't feel wanted or supported, or they are forced to leave, many teachers of color don't last long.

As much as trainings, conferences, and research can educate white teachers on racism, teachers of color have real life experience that white teachers will never understand. They can provide input based on personal experience rather than rely on what they've been taught, and because of their identity, it's easier for them to incorporate talks about racism in classes than it is for white teachers. They educate students from their perspective which is more impactful and accurate than a white teacher's perspective. White teachers can make efforts to become more thoughtful on what they teach in classes, and try to create representation for their students, but a teacher of color embodies that representation. Because teachers play such a critical role in education and shaping the next generation, they need to be compensated fairly for the work that I'm asking them to do.

Another positive aspect of having teachers of color is that they are more receptive when you bring them concerns about racism involving other students in the class. When I've tried to bring racism up to white teachers, they've brushed it off and empathized with the student who made a racist comment rather than me. It's like they don't understand the significance and impact of racism. In contrast, when I've brought concerns to teachers of color, they immediately assure me that they will take care of it and that they know how serious it is. They do a better job at shutting down racism when it occurs in class discussions, and make sure they educate the student who made the comment. I've had white teachers practically encourage racist views to be discussed in their class among white students who don't know what they are talking about. Race should be spoken about, but racist ideas shouldn't be entertained as a reasonable view to have.

Whiteness is already centralized within American society, and the lack of a representative education teaches that directly to the youth. Curriculum needs to be representative of all people to remove its roots in whiteness. Students of color and other marginalized students need to be taught about their own backgrounds, identities, and communities. White students need to be taught that there are other people and cultures out there they need to be aware of and respect because the world is bigger than only white people. Beyond the curriculum, resources at schools should represent the needs of all students, not just white, cisgender, heterosexual, able-bodied students. I focus mostly on racism in my reflection, but no marginalized group of people is getting the representation and resources in school that they need and deserve.

Ignorance

Starting my junior year, I enrolled in Running Start, a program where I take my classes at the local community college rather than at my high school for both college credit and high school credit. First quarter I took English 101, and it was the first non-Eurocentric English class I'd ever taken. We read and wrote about essays that touched on topics of racism, gender and social inequities, and none of my previous English classes had focused on these topics. The authors we read pieces from were people of color coming from many different backgrounds. We had interesting discussions that dove beneath the surface, so I was generally engaged and excited about doing work for that class.

Even though we had a representative curriculum, my teacher was unsurprisingly a white woman; all my previous English teachers had been white women as well. I went into this class with some background information on this teacher. One of my friends, also a young black woman, had felt targeted in the same teacher's class a year before. She had been one of the only black students in this class, which was the same situation I was in. Knowing this, I was especially attuned to any possible discrimination. None occurred after weeks, and I hoped that she had improved from the last year. Maybe she had talked to someone or gone through training.

We were well into the quarter, and I just turned in one of my favorite essays I have ever written; it's an essay comparing me to another black woman, and I analyze the differences in how we each navigated society as black women. One piece of this essay compares how we each responded to ignorance. As I have become increasingly racially and socially critical, ignorance is not something I take lightly, and I no longer put up with it as I did when I was younger. I outlined my response to ignorance in this essay which can be summed up in a few steps. First, I take a step back from the situation. Second, during this time away from the situation, whether that be for a few minutes, an hour, or days, I collect my thoughts and cool down. Third, I approach the perpetuator and explain my thoughts. Finally, I allow them to make their decision on whether they want to open their minds to new information, or if they want to remain in the same mindset as before. I allow them to make this decision because even though I do feel that I can educate people, it is not my job to force anyone to change their mind.

A few days after I had turned in this essay, we were watching a video of James Baldwin being interviewed to prepare for our next paper. From what I remember, he was answering a question on why he moved from New York to Paris. In his answer, he explained that he moved because if someone called him a nigger one more time, he would kill someone, or he would end up dead himself. James Baldwin, a black man, has every right to use that word. The word has been used against him, and he was explaining the impact that the word had on him. My white English teacher, on the other hand, has no right to use the word, even if she was quoting the Baldwin video that we had just watched. Yet, that was exactly what happened. With no hesitation, the word slipped off her tongue and into the air.

I could feel the atmosphere in the class changing. In my head, I was still processing what had just happened. Another girl in my class was the first to say something. She began by saying how it was inappropriate for a white woman to use that word. My teacher immediately launched into her explanation that consisted of poor excuses: "I was only quoting Baldwin," "I wanted to make sure everyone knew what he had said." Unsurprisingly, she became defensive, a common trait found in white people due to internalized racial superiority. I could see straight through her defensiveness and right to the ignorance that was at its core. These situations aren't new to me. I had my plan of attack memorized; the first step being exit the situation. In no way would I be able to focus or gain anything else out of the class that day, so I packed up my stuff and walked to the door. As I was leaving, my teacher asked me if I was sure I did not want to stay to discuss it. My response was simply, "Not today." Step one had been completed.

I was now moving into step two; gathering information and collecting my thoughts. I talked to friends, teachers, and other students in the class. However, the most impactful conversation I had was with my therapist. I especially wanted to talk to him about it because he is also black, but closer to the age of my teacher. He advised me to talk to her, which I was already planning on doing, and to first listen to her before I explained my point of view. He said that understanding where your opponent is coming from is the best way to get through to them. I was told to not assume where she is coming from, but to ask her and listen. In all honesty, I could not have cared less where she was coming from. I wanted to tell her my thoughts, but listening to hers was not part of the plan. But when I thought about it, I knew that I would be more likely to listen to someone who had listened to me first. I knew what I believed; white people should not use the n-word because of the word's history, and the power associated with it. I assumed that she believed that because she was using it in an academic setting while quoting James Baldwin it was acceptable. Even though I was certain that this was her justification, it would not hurt to ask.

Step two had been completed, so I asked her to meet with me after class to talk. She had already apologized to me and to the class through an email, but I still felt the need to meet with her one on one. I met her in her office, and the first thing she said to me was that she was sorry. She explained how she had talked to many people about the situation, including the dean, in order to have an understanding. Through talking to people, she had concluded that younger people were generally against white people using the n-word in any way, while older people were generally accepting of it in certain scenarios. She explained how she understood that using the word as a white woman today was still controversial, and with her class being primarily young people, she should be more cautious. She reiterated how she never would use the word in any other scenario; she was simply quoting Baldwin.

I was surprised at how much time and effort I saved by letting her talk first. I had come prepared, ready to explain my opinion to her, but from what she had said, she already had heard what I would have said from other people. She basically had done my work for me. I expressed my appreciation for her self-reflection, and gave her some insight from where I was standing, also explaining how it would be inappropriate to use the word in any setting and in front of anyone. Step three was done, and it seemed the answer to step four was she was willing to educate herself.

Ignorance has become a buzzword that people tend to throw into conversations of race and equity. Being ignorant is a fear for many people because of how the term is used. Ignorance means simply means "a lack of knowledge or information." If that is the case, everyone must be ignorant; there is no one who knows everything. However, when this word is used today, it is likely referring to a lack of social awareness. Even still, many people who claim to be "woke" are still socially unaware in at least one area. Therefore, I find the term ignorance to be a bit problematic in the way that it is used today. It creates an "in-crowd" and an "out-crowd," and pushes people out of conversations if they do not already know everything. Because anyone can be ignorant in one way or another, it is the responsibility of everyone to help everyone gain the information that we lack. Of course, there are people who have chosen to be socially unaware and hold their ground with those views. These people are not ignorant because they have the knowledge or access to it, but they are making a choice to refute it.

There are ignorant people of all races. Ignorant does not mean racist; it only means having a lack of knowledge. People can be ignorant about gender, religion, mental health and so many other things, but for my purposes, I'm going to focus on racial ignorance. The true racially ignorant people are the ones who have no knowledge, or incorrect knowledge, on issues of race. These people make up most of society. They may mean no harm, but their words and actions can still be harmful. They have good intent, and still a negative impact. People of color are less likely to be racially ignorant because they live through racism and inequity. White people have a higher tendency to be racially ignorant because their own experiences do not teach them as much. School has racially ignorant people just like anywhere else. From misinformation to microaggressions to blatant racism; students of color face it all. As students, the largest influencer of our experience are our teachers and the other students around us, so ignorance based in discrimination and racism from them is a common occurrence.

> *"In public school a lot of people were more aware of current racial issues. In private school everyone is sheltered; they all come from white backgrounds. That's who they've been going to school with, and that's who they're surrounded with. Throw me into the mix, and they're not really educated on how to interact with me, not that they must interact with me any differently. They're scared of everything and they don't want to talk about a lot of things."*

Up until and even after high school, there are students who have been sheltered from knowledge about race. They likely know the common stereotypes, what they absorb from the media, and what they learn from their environment, but white people have the privilege to be unaware of racial relations. It doesn't stand out to them daily the way it does for people of color. When they are forced to face the fact that race and racism are real, and they are upholding it, it can be hard for them to adjust. They often lash out in defense, or start to become excessively emotional which is hard for students of color to navigate. I remember the first time I caused a white girl to cry because I told her that as a white person, whether she claimed she wasn't racist or not, she was racist because she is directly benefiting off racist systems. My intention wasn't to make her cry, it was to tell her the truth, and she responded by crying. I believe that any emotion is valid, but in that situation, she was trying to villainize me by acting like I attacked her.

> *"During black lives matter week, a white girl in my history class stood up and asked why slavery was still relevant today, and why she was responsible for what happened in the past. When I called her out and tried to explain the role slavery has on the social hierarchy we have today, she listened to me for less than a minute before cutting me off. Another student, who was also a person of color, attempted to explain the concept as well, but received the same treatment as I did. Finally, when a white student spoke up; the girl listened patiently. She was still confused after this ordeal, so I had to tell her straight up that an example of slavery's role today is the way she listened to and valued the voice of a fellow white peer while she felt inclined to ignore the voices of people of color. She retaliated with asking, 'are you calling me racist?' I thought she was displaying a microaggression with no malicious intent, but the way she challenged what I was saying and took my calm explanation as an insult just shows the racist elements of the education*

system that happens every day. These events
happen so fast and don't look like a big deal,
but they add up to create a foundation for
the unsafe environment for people of color."

Having to call out white students in an all-white class is hard. Even as outspoken as I am, there are times when I am too tired to call out every racist comment that I hear. I do my best, but there are other things I need to put my energy into, such as passing the class, shocking! I also have the privilege of being more comfortable speaking out in white classrooms because I was in the honors program for years. Many people I talked with would not feel comfortable at all. Therefore, it's especially important for teachers to pay attention to what is going on in their class, and have the skills to intervene, so that the burden doesn't solely fall on students of color.

People respond to ignorance in a variety of ways, and it shifts depending on the situation. The last few years, especially on social media, "cancel culture" has become common. Cancel culture is a no-tolerance approach where if someone does or says something "wrong," usually ignorant, they are cancelled. Being cancelled means that people are done with them, want to make them irrelevant, and refuse to provide them a chance to redeem themselves. For abusers and rapists, like Chris Brown and Kodak Black, I fully believe their careers should have ended long ago, and their platforms should be taken away, but people continue to make up excuses for them that they don't deserve. I feel similarly towards people who are repeatedly racist; they should not have their platform because they are refusing to acknowledge or learn from mistakes. My views start to shift when someone makes a mistake that's out of ignorance. One thing I said

92

earlier in this chapter was that I disagree with having an in-crowd and an out-crowd which ties to this. Cancelling someone for acting from ignorance is counterproductive because it pushes them directly into the "out-crowd" without giving them the chance to learn, and potentially shift their views.

On social media and in real life interactions, like in class, we can choose to either call-out people on their ignorance, or call-in people. Calling someone out is simply telling them what they said was wrong, and it usually is not followed by an explanation and doesn't allow the perpetuator to gain understanding. In fact, it can make them stray even further away because they feel attacked, confused, or frustrated. Calling someone in is telling someone what they did wrong, why it was wrong, and allowing them to respond. It can open a dialogue that both people can contribute to and come out of with further understanding. I'm not going to tell students of color what to do because it's not anyone's place to dictate. I personally do both, usually depending on how much energy I have, how important it is to me, and who the person is. Calling people in can be exhausting, especially when they shut themselves off from what they're being told. I always follow my rule of letting them make the choice to listen and learn or not. It's not my job to explain something to someone who refuses to listen, especially when what they are saying is hurtful and disrespectful.

> *"Holding friends accountable is the best thing that white students can do. There are a lot of problematic white students, but there are also those who notice the racism. If they were to call each other out, it would*

relieve pressure from students of color."

"My history teacher made a good example of white people being accomplices instead of allies. An accomplice is there to help you, to get involved and to be attached to the struggle."

I know that there are white students out there who want to make class a safer place for their peers. I see them, and I urge them to push themselves to do even better. White students hold a certain power that students of color do not. In order to be a white advocate, they must be educated themselves, and work to educate others. Calling people in relieves students of color from always having to take on that task. Step up even when it is uncomfortable, and step back when asked to. Holding your friends accountable can make a huge difference and creates a ripple effect for others to do the same. Even when there aren't any people of color around to witness it, calling out friends on their racism is important to make it clear that racism shouldn't be tolerated. Silence is compliance.

"A lot of students at my school can be insensitive. One time I was eating Asian food at school because I'm Asian. A guy asked me if I was eating dog. I was disgusted, I have a dog and I would never eat one."

"A lot of the racist comments in classes are more so structured to be race jokes. White people shouldn't make them, and they

come off as ignorant. People usually laugh
it off and not take it seriously. It happens
a lot, and it's uncomfortable. When I call
it out, people don't take you seriously, but
if I don't say anything, I'm upholding it."

Stereotypical jokes make up a lot of the racism found in classrooms. However, racism is not any different with a punchline. Racist jokes perpetuate racism in classes, and allow racist ideology to continue. They are not harmless. Growing up, I had speech issues which caused my voice to have a slight accent that people thought was funny. Kids on my bus would laugh at me, saying I sounded like I was from Africa. They clearly didn't know what African accents sound like, and I am not from Africa, so they only said that because I'm black. This is another opportunity for white students to step up and say something. A simple, "That's not funny" could make them think twice about making one of those jokes again. But no need to stop there, report them if it continues because racism should not be tolerated.

My school had a well-known group of male neo-Nazis who ran Instagram accounts that were filled with horrific anti-sematic, racist, sexist, and overall disgusting memes. Yes, memes. When people at my school found out about this, people were sent into a frenzy. A lot of people couldn't believe that people at "such a woke school" could have these views. I was horrified by what I saw on their accounts, but wasn't at all surprised that they went to my school. All sorts of racist ideologies were upheld by so many people at the school, and it didn't seem shocking that some of them were bold enough to post about those ideas. They claimed innocence, and said that it was supposed to be funny which I expected, and faced no consequences from the school.

> *"In group projects, white students don't think I'll do as much or hold my part. They aren't being blatantly racist, but still aren't treating us as equals."*

Microaggressions are normalized comments, actions, and attitudes that can be intentional or unintentional and are based on prejudice towards any marginalized group. These make up a large part of my experience with ignorance in school. Microaggressions can be intentional, which means they are not based on ignorance, but often they are unintentional and based fully on ignorance. It could be as simple as a table partner double checking my work when I offer an answer, but not checking the work of their white table partners. Or, if I have a different answer or idea than a white student, they will go with the answer of the white student even if I explain how I am correct. They do not believe in my abilities unless a white student or the teacher agrees with me.

Sometimes ignorance comes in the form of comments on appearance, such as "your hair is so weird" or "your eyes are small." Whatever it is, it hurts. Ignorance may be innocent and without malice, but it still has a victim. Beyond the individual victim, it feeds into and upholds racist ideology which is prevalent in American society and has been used to marginalize people of color. The normalization of racial ignorance has allowed people to make light of it, putting students of color in a difficult situation where they might not be sure whether they're allowed to be angry about it or not. For instance, in my yoga class during the spring of junior year, I came in with a freshly bleached buzz cut and was complimented by a white guy in my class. The compliment itself was fine, but then he went on to say that it looked good with my skin tone, "even though it looks like you got darker." I was so caught off guard, and wasn't sure if I was correct in interpreting it as a weird comment. The more I thought about it, the more uncomfortable it made me, and I came to realize that even though it was likely unintentional, and he was unaware of the way it was received, it still was a microaggression.

> *"In my literature class we spent an entire month on the question 'what does it mean to be black in America?' If you can imagine, it was me answering questions for the black community which is not something that I wanted to do, and not something that I think I can do. There were times where I felt people being careful around me. You could tell that all eyes were on me for a lot of the time, and that made me uncomfortable and tired because I felt like I always had to be on guard."*

> *"Especially when topics of race come up in the classroom, I'm always looked upon as someone who automatically knows more about the subject because of my race. It singles me out, and it's happened multiple times."*

Students of color should be given more space during discussions about race, but putting them on the spot is uncomfortable.

No black person can speak for the entire black community, and it is ignorant to think that they can. Especially in school, it is a problem to have one student be the designated race encyclopedia. Teachers should be providing other ways to gain an understanding on race. It is an important subject to be taught and discussed; diving into it helps everyone gain an understanding, and allows racially ignorant students to learn. Race is a hard subject to be taught and discussed, and having the discussions in the wrong way can be harmful for students of color. The discussions must be well facilitated by the teacher; correcting ignorance, shutting racism down, and getting the discussion back on track are important to maintain a safe environment for the discussion. Trust me, it is not fun to find out half the people in your class are incredibly racist and then watch them be allowed to loudly express those ideas. Teachers should be required to have knowledge on race, but it's important for white teachers to realize that they will never have the same understanding the people of color do, including their students.

> *"I don't talk to many people who have been in the honors program just because in middle school I had some bad experiences and heard that honors kids have said disrespectful things about the general program. In my Spanish class, a mixed program class, there was one white APP boy and he said something like, 'I don't know why there's so many general students in this class, I don't like it'. It made me wonder what was wrong with the general kids, because I was one of them. There's a tie with disliking general*

program kids and disliking people of color.
Many people of color were in general, not
because we weren't smart enough, but
because some of us didn't have access to
take the test or didn't even know about it."

Segregation of students leaves room for ignorance. There are assumptions made about both programs. However, since the white honors program has more power, it is worse when they are making assumptions about the general program. I heard many negative comments about the general program when I was in honors, and all of it came from a place of total ignorance. They had no idea who they were talking about or if it was even true. When a program full of white students is talking down on a program full of students of color, racism is involved. It might be unintended and come from ignorance, but the impact feeds into racism. The comments I heard about kids in the general program matched directly with stereotypes about black and brown people. They were often called loud, dumb, and disruptive. Even though the general students would call the students in honors potentially hurtful names like in nerds, suck-ups, annoying, and other names along those lines, they had no racial basis, and were based off them being in a higher-level program.

It is unrealistic to attempt to remove all ignorance from the education system because ignorance is in every aspect of society. However, we should take steps towards that. In schools we can focus on diminishing the amount of racial ignorance through racial education and calling people in. Schools are the obvious place to educate people, and racism is an important topic for society to be educated on. There is no excuse to not providing inclusive and representative education to students because not only does it enrich the class for students of color, it also forces white students and teachers to face their ignorance.

Treatment

I went into Junior year excited to take sociology through Running Start. Finally, a class that suited some of my interests. I was eager to learn and take as much out of the class as I could. The first day of class I wanted to make a good impression. I walked up to my professor, introduced myself, and told him how excited I was to be taking his class. He seemed nice enough, however it is key for me to mention that he was a white man. Even with my view that all white people are inherently racist, I hate to solely judge how someone will treat me because they are white, though I will be a little more cautious. My first impression was correct at first, he continued to be nice and I learned a lot in his class during those first few weeks.

The midterm was when things began to shift between the two of us. For the midterm, the class would be watching the film "American Me," and analyzing it sociologically. I was fine with this assignment, until on the Friday before the week we'd be viewing the film, he decided to mention for the first time that the film had graphic rape scenes. My experiences with sexual assault, including one only a month before, made this assignment inaccessible for me because of how badly it could trigger me. Right after class, I went up to him and tried to voice my concerns. He attempted to minimize them off by saying we'd be skipping over some of the more graphic scenes. He said he would talk about them to the class, but the students would have a limited dialogue on those scenes. Still, this was not something I felt safe doing because of how it could trigger panic and potentially a relapse. When I told him that, he seemed confused and annoyed with my request.

The whole weekend, between the Friday that I found out the content of the film, and the Monday where we would begin watching it, I had terrible anxiety and panic. I knew I would not be able to make it through watching the film, and I hated that my trauma would cause me to fail. Monday morning of the midterm, I came to class early to try to talk to him again. I was already nervous because I knew I would have to explain my experiences for him to take it more seriously. Before I could even say anything, he snapped at me for bothering him and was incredibly rude. I started to feel a panic attack coming and left the room as I was starting to break down. I could not believe how insensitive he was being towards me over something that was a legitimate concern of mine, and I had never seen him treat anyone else in the class that way. I talked to a few people who I trusted and decided to message him asking to make a meeting to talk about the situation. I dreaded going to this meeting because of how terrible talking to him made me feel. He was snappy, inconsiderate, and demeaning, but by the end of the meeting he gave me an alternative midterm assignment, so my goal had been accomplished.

I thought that things between us would go back to normal; I was wrong. After the midterm situation, he became increasingly hostile towards me. It was a bad time for this to start because I was going through a tough time with a self-harm relapse and suicidality. I was scared to ask questions or ask for help even though I was struggling. Finally, I decided to make a meeting with him to clear up some questions I had in the class. The meeting went surprisingly well, and I thought I had a hold on the class for the rest of the quarter. He told me what assignments were due in the future, and which ones I could make up for partial credit after missing class because of mental health reasons. I did everything he told me to do and turned it in when he said it was due. I did not foresee any future problems.

A few weeks after this meeting, I got sick. I emailed him the night before class, as the syllabus said to do, and asked him if I should come or not because an assignment was due that day. He wrote back, telling me to get better soon and to just check in with my group because it was a group project, and to bring my other assignments when I returned. I checked in with my group as he asked, and I thought it had been handled. I came to class thirty minutes early after two days of being sick in order to talk to him and turn my assignments in. He barely even let me get a word out before he started lecturing me on my irresponsibility. He refused to listen to anything I had to say, continuing to talk over me anytime I tried to speak. He told me that I should've had this done weeks ago, when at our previous meeting he told me it was due two days ago, the day I was sick. My shock started to turn into anger, he was purposely trying to screw me over, and refused to admit that he might be in the wrong. I had done nothing except for what he had asked me to do, and now he wouldn't even let me explain that.

Of all the things I wanted to say to him, I chose the kindest, "I am so done with white people." Because I was, and it was the truth, I was done being looked down on as inferior, irresponsible, and lazy. I had worked my ass off in that class and was being treated like I was trying to scam my way through. The look on his face when I said that was truly worth all of it. He looked like he was about to shit his pants. The few other people in the class were silent for that one, precious moment. Then, he ruined it by telling me I needed to go talk to the dean about what I said, and I would likely no longer be in that class.

I fought the urge to laugh in his face. Him, a sociology professor, someone who I would assume to have a solid understanding of racism, was acting like the victim. A white man kicked me out of his class because I voiced that I was being treated unfairly. I thought it was hilarious, truly hilarious. It became even funnier when he said to me "You need to talk to the dean about your racist comments." Racist? Let me take a step back for a second. Racist. A white man kicked me out because I voiced that I was being treated unfairly. As he should know as a sociology professor, racism is prejudice plus power. If anyone needs a refresher, white people hold the power in this society, therefore on no grounds can I be racist towards him, or any other white person. There was no way I was going to let someone who believed that a black person can be racist towards a white person teach me sociology, especially not anything about race and ethnicity which was the next unit. That was the moment I decided to receive no credit for the class instead of continuing to endure that environment. Even though he was in the wrong, I was the one who was negatively impacted in the situation. I had put a lot of work into the class for nearly a whole quarter, and it was all going to waste. The teacher got off with no consequences, and is still getting to teach sociology without an understanding of racism, probably screwing over a few other students of color along the way.

Teachers have the most direct power over the success of students in their class. Family life, social aspects, the system, and personal problems play a huge role as well, but the teachers have an overarching authority. When teachers are actively racially biased, the success among students becomes skewed. In many classes I've been in that have both white students and students of color, the white students are doing better in the class. Students have little power to hold their teachers accountable, and often are forced to cope with racism in classes instead of being able to make changes. While some may only pay attention to bad treatment in the form of explicit racism, I think that bias and microaggressions are just as impactful on a student's success in the class.

"There's definitely a bias in the classroom towards white people. When I call for a teacher, nothing. That white dude next to me calls for a teacher, 'Oh yea, Timmy, I can help you with this and that.' Teachers gravitate towards them more in the classroom."

"The only black people in my honors pre-calculus class are my friend and me. It was fine in the beginning, but around the second month of school I got this vibe that I shouldn't be in that classroom. The teacher would make comments that suggested it. I'd be working on an assignment and ask a question, she'd say that if I don't know I shouldn't be in the class. Even when we just started the unit, and obviously I'd have

questions. Recently she pulled me aside and said I should drop that class. I wasn't going to drop the class, I need it as a requirement, but I asked why. She told me I wasn't trying hard enough and only socialized. That pissed me off because there'd been many incidents up to that when I'd be sitting down and the only reason I'd be talking is to ask someone how to do something. She'd yell at me and call me disrespectful while there's a white student jumping off the table, screaming. I confronted her and told her that she was targeting me, I wasn't subtle about it, I told her I felt targeted and I wanted her to stop. She just repeated that I should drop the class."

"When white students are having a rough time, teachers are kind and allow them to take care of themselves. Students of color do not receive the same treatment, I'm not getting the same leeway. I feel like I'm held up to a high standard. White girls get the best treatment from teachers. They're white, so they already have that privilege. Teachers see them as small and helpless, which comes from sexism, so they try to take care of them. This ends up with white girls receiving special treatment."

When teachers spend more time with their white students than their students of color, it sends a clear message to students of color that they aren't as important in the class. This can lead to a lack of effort in a class, and the feeling of unimportance. More direct than that, if a black student is asking for help and doesn't receive it, they won't understand the material as well. Because of this, students of color fail or do worse in classes more often than the white students. Providing extra help is part of a teacher's job, not a burden, and even if they have explained it before, there's no reason to be rude or condescending about it. Telling a student that they should drop the class before offering any suggestions for them to do better is taking the easy route as a teacher. If a student is continuing to do poorly in a class, a teacher's first instinct should be to work with them to see if things can be changed to give them more success in the class. If that does not work, maybe it is the wrong class level for them, but telling a student to drop a class because of socializing and presumed lack of effort is putting all responsibility on the student.

White students are given more privileges in classes. Teachers, from my experience and what my peers have shared, cater towards white girls in classes. They tend to be called on more in discussions which leads to the decline of participation from students of color. All the "teacher's pets" that I have known were white girls. I have also noticed that white male teachers cater to white girls more than white female teachers do. This stems from the sexism that causes men to see women as needing more attention than men. White male teachers baby their white girl students, giving them extra attention and support that helps them succeed. This treatment is gross and problematic in its own way, and I've heard many white girls speak out about feeling uncomfortable around their male teachers because of weird comments and excessive touching. As someone who presented as a girl for most of my life, I have had these experiences as well, and have felt sexualized by my male teachers, but was not getting the lenience that white girls receive. I don't want to diminish misogyny, but it's a fact that race plays into it, and women of color have a different experience than white women.

"Teachers don't stop students' racism. In a lot of my classes there's been a group of white male students who make a crack about slavery or something. Instead of doing anything, the teacher said we should respect everyone's opinion. The teachers aren't doing anything racist, but not holding students accountable is racist."

"I had a teacher this year who would consistently call me by the wrong name, the name of the only other black girl in the class. The teacher constantly mixed us up, no matter how many times we corrected him. He even admitted, 'Yeah, it's because of your guys' race.'"

Back in my AP chemistry class, me and my friend who is Filipinx were the extent of the color in that room. For most of the course we joked about it together and got through it. Earlier that year there had been a schoolwide "Black Lives Matter Week", which all teachers were expected to plan activities and discussions for. The teacher of this class did not do anything for this event, with the excuse that the AP test was coming up and we had to get through all the material. So now that it was after the AP test, we had time to make up for the "Black Lives Matter Week" that we had missed previously. My friend suggested this, but my teacher dismissed it as too complicated and hard to pull off well. I felt myself fuming inside and I knew I needed to cool off before I decided how to respond. I went on my phone to distract myself and let my heart rate come down. After my teacher said to me, "Azure, it looks like you're on your phone," I snapped and in front of the whole class said, "Well, it looks like you don't care about black people." The look on his face was priceless and the class became dead silent.

He asked both me and my friend to come outside to talk with him, as if we were the representatives black students.. He then suggested that we work with him to build an activity that has to do with the Black Lives Matter Theme. My friend, told him straight up "I'm not black so it's not my place to do this." My teacher said something like, "I know, but you have a clear interest and knowledge on this topic." It struck me how hard he was trying to lump us together as ambassadors for the cause. It was also irresponsible that he expected us to do all the work for this when he should have been doing it in the first place; allowing us to do it under his supervision doesn't take away from the fact that he wasn't planning on doing anything at all. We didn't have the energy to do his job for him.

The next year, I decided to pay a visit to his AP physics class, and asked him point blank if he was planning anything for the Black Lives Matter week that year. I could tell I caught him off guard and he started rambling that he'd been thinking about it and had some ideas, but wanted it to be a collaborative process that involved the students in the class. I looked around the room, and asked if there were any black students in the class, to which his response was, "That would be negatory." I told him that because there were no black students in the class, he needed to find a way to create the activities on his own time with the input of black people for it to be effective, and walked out to leave him to figure it out.

"I was in a math class my freshman year with mostly white kids and a white teacher. After the first test, the teacher brought me out and accused me of cheating. During the test, I was sitting in between these two white girls and she said, 'I have a feeling that you were looking at their papers.' I started crying when she brought me out there. I was just trying to do my test, I did not cheat. I had the same answer as one of the girls and they were both wrong, but I just got it wrong and she also got it wrong in the same way. It was a simple math error, but she assumed I cheated off the white girl, and not that she could have cheated off me. I didn't register if that was about race at first but as I thought about it more, it seems like it was and that sucks."

"I went to my English class to turn in my final essay. My teacher looked at it and told me she couldn't accept it because it didn't look like my writing and she assumed I plagiarized it. When I asked for clarification, I was told that the writing was 'too good' to be mine. A little bit of background, I came into that class knowing

nothing about writing. I learned so much in that class, and my style has changed so much. I took what she taught and incorporated it into my essay. I was crying explaining that it was my work, but she wouldn't believe me."

"I had the same history teacher for Freshman and Sophomore year. All the tests we did I didn't do great on, but I didn't fail them either. I would meet with him and ask what I did wrong. For almost every question we went over he would say he didn't remember why he took off points. I was confused why he was taking points off for no reason. In comparison to white classmates' tests, I had much lower scores."

Teachers obviously have control over student's grades. Racially biased teachers extend their bias into their grading, hurting student's grades who are not white because of it. I have had a lot of experiences where a white classmate and I would have the same answer on a test, but I was marked down. It happens especially in English and History classes because correct test answers can be more than one idea or interpretation. If my classmates and I were trying to convey the same idea, the teacher would grade the white student's answer as thought out well, but mine was graded like I had no idea what I was talking about. If a student does feel comfortable enough to tell their teacher that they feel targeted, this should be addressed, not ignored. When students are not given any power, it runs the risk of further mistreatment and misconduct in classes. Knowing that they will be held to high standards will push teachers to take note of their bias and improve their practices.

> *"When I was a freshman, I had a language arts teacher who was very condescending. The way he talked to me, the tone of voice and his body language were different from how he was with the white kids. I wish teachers wouldn't treat students of color differently. Acknowledge our differences but don't let it be a handicap. I wish I was treated equally to white students."*

There is a difference between adjusting the class to suit the needs of all students and blatantly treating students of different races differently. Students of color are there to learn and do well just like the white students are. Yes, it is difficult to be a person of color in our society and people of color face challenges that white people never will. However, we are just as driven, or lazy, as white students, and we have the same intelligence too. There is no reason to believe otherwise. The adjustments should be made by having a representative curriculum, correcting ignorance, stopping discrimination and giving space to students of color. It does not mean speaking slowly, assuming we need help, or any other way of being condescending. If a student has an accessibility need, that is a different reason for individual adjustments; it should not be defined by their race. Again, it is important for students to feel comfortable calling their teacher out on their bias, so that we have the power to hold them accountable.

"When I was in seventh grade, my math teacher said something along the lines of, 'Go back on the boat you came from.' I didn't know what that meant back then. When I found out, I couldn't believe my math teacher of all people said this. He was an old white guy, he was racist and sexist, but everyone loved him since they thought he was funny."

"My teacher took my final paper and scribbled all over it in red pen in front of the whole class while saying how awful it was after I said how proud I was to prove a point. The same teacher referred to me as 'pretty but dumb.'"

"Junior year, I was attending a school in the north end of Seattle. When I was about to transfer to a school in the south end. I received a lot of backlash from my teacher. He would say off color comments about me going to a south end school and 'those people' that would be there. It was an uncomfortable situation."

At my school, I see four different categories of teachers. There are the white teachers who are blatantly racist, and known for it, the teachers who are people of color trying their best to make a positive impact, "neutral" teachers who are complacent, and the white teachers who view themselves as superior because they've deluded themselves and others into thinking that they are allies for students of color. The last type of teacher I mentioned is the most challenging for me to deal with; they are more subtle, just as harmful as blatantly racist teachers, and use their perceived image as an ally to deflect any criticism.

Junior year, I was part of an social justice club at my school that is led by upperclassman, that holds retreats throughout the year. They focus on looking at issues through racial lenses, building community, and personal growth. The year I was on staff, I worked with a group of nine other students, and the group was almost entirely black students. We had two advisors, one was a black woman, but the one who dominated was a white man who was loved by the school and seen as "one of the good ones." He's the one I will be referring to throughout this section. I had no prior experiences with him, so I went into the club thinking that he would be great to work with because of what I had heard about him. For the first few months, he seemed like a good guy, but did make a few remarks that were questionable to me and a few others in the group. We all tried to ignore it because we needed him as an advisor, and usually he was good to work with. I genuinely trusted him, and I even asked him for help on this book a while back. He was one of the few adults at my school that I felt safe going to for support.

That winter, directly after I had been raped and was being attacked by my best friends and boyfriend about it, I needed support. I went to his class after school because I didn't know where else to go. I told him everything that had happened, from the rape, to the backlash, to how suicidal I was, to how horrible my nightmares were, and how I couldn't sleep without smoking weed. He listened, and talking to him made me feel better for a moment. We talked for a while until he had convinced me I should admit myself to the hospital that night. He gave me his number, and told me I could call whenever. I really appreciated the support he gave to me during that dark time. I refused to go into the school building for the next few months, so I didn't see him until the next retreat.

We left for the retreat with a group of around seventy campers, ten chaperones, and our two advisors. The first retreat had been somewhat of a letdown, so all of us were counting on this one going well. For trips to be allowed by the school, they have a strict no-substance policy. We were instructed by our advisors to tell campers that if they gave it up on the first night, it would be kept confidential and they would not get in trouble. On the first night, we were confronted with an issue: someone on the trip had brought a dab pen, a vaping device used with cannabis oil. One of the people on staff had walked in on the person using it, and took it. She immediately brought it to attention to our advisors and the rest of staff. The person using the dab pen explained that they brought it to help them sleep because they had PTSD. I immediately empathized with them because I was in the same place. The only reason the camper handed it over was that they were promised they would not be in trouble, and their name would stay out of it. Since that was what we told them, none of us were willing to break our promise and tell our advisors who it was. Before our advisors came in to talk to us, we all agreed that we would keep it confidential.

Our advisor barged in soon after. He started berating us about the situation, and attempted to shame us into giving up the name because it could shut down the whole program for good if we didn't. We watched him throw a temper tantrum and accuse us all for being irresponsible by telling the campers incorrect information about the drug policy even though he told us to say what we said. We attempted to explain that the person was using the dab pen because they needed it to sleep, which we should take into consideration, and he angrily retorted that if they needed weed, they shouldn't have come. My heart sank in my chest because he was being incredibly insensitive to people with mental illness, and disregarding everything I had told him about my own struggles. I started to see a version of him that I ignored previously. After we held our ground for long enough, he angrily left. All of us wanted to give him the benefit of the doubt, but we were frustrated with what he was saying. Everyone was upset, drained, and irritable, so we decided to finish talking the next morning.

The group of staff met with our advisor after breakfast to negotiate. He immediately jumped into a rant about our irresponsibility and how ashamed we should be about putting the program at risk. We tried to explain our reasoning, but he refused to listen. I ended up snapping at him for his bullshit and he stormed out. I was pissed that he refused to take partial blame because he advised us to tell campers we would keep it confidential, and I was still hurt about what he said the night before.

The rest of the trip, staff was on our own. Our advisor refused to participate, or even speak to most of us. He spent most of his time sulking in a corner, and talking shit about the group to the other chaperones and students. We were all stressed out about the future of the program while working to make it the best experience possible for the campers. As the trip went on, I slowly heard bits and pieces of information from other staff members about what he was saying. It turned out that he said he hated the program, hated working with us because we had ideas he opposed, and that this was not the job he signed up for. It wasn't hard for us to realize that he didn't know that the group he would be working with would be predominantly black because in previous years the staff had been very white. He never cared about the program, he only cared about himself. After hearing all that, I was fuming. I was tired of this white man masquerading around as an ally when his actions went against us, and everything we had been fighting for. I felt like I had been lied to by him, and our relationship was nothing to him.

After all my bad experiences with teachers, specifically white men, it's become hard for me to trust them. It's difficult for students of color to demand better treatment and higher standards of their teachers because it's structured so that we have little power. It impacts more than our grade; it can impact how we feel about education, the work we put in, and how we view ourselves. When we are constantly looked down on by our teachers, it's hard to not begin thinking of ourselves in that way. We deserve to feel valued by our teachers, and see ourselves in a positive way. Teachers who work to be unbiased and support their students make a huge difference in our experiences. It's important for teachers to show their students that they have flaws, and are comfortable listening to feedback. Students should be able to hold their teachers accountable for their actions when they are unjust. When teachers are free to do as they wish without repercussions, students of color are at risk.

Discipline

It was May, just over a month before school would end, when my school decided to enforce a dress code that had seldom been enforced before. The day it happened I probably heard from ten different people that the administration was going down the halls dress coding one person after the next. I thought it was ridiculous. Imagine the confusion when a dress code is implemented seven months into the year, without any warning. I saw no need for a dress code, as they do more harm than good, and there is no need to police the bodies of underage students unless they are breaking a nudity law or being discriminatory. After seeing who was getting dress coded, and who wasn't, it was clear that because of racial bias, there was unequal enforcement. Teachers, administration and security at my school had a bias against black and brown girls and students from the queer community. Though I heard many stories of marginalized students receiving unfair dress code discipline that day, I'll only share my own.

The dress code started being enforced on a Friday, and on

the following Monday, the temperature was predicted to be over eighty degrees. For me, that's boiling hot. Dress code or not, there was no way I was going to wear something to school that I'd be uncomfortable in. I went to school in shorts, a strapless top, and a jacket, and it was something that I'd seen people wear at school before. I got through first and second period with no issues. Third period, it got interesting. My teacher told me that if I took off my jacket, I'd have to go to the office. Well, I was hot, the room had no ventilation, and I could feel my body temperature rising. I took my jacket off to cool down. I looked around the room and saw many other girls in the class breaking the "dress code" in a similar way. The only difference was, they were all white and didn't have the curves or skin color that made my outfit "inappropriate." Immediately, my teacher walked over to me and told me I had to go to the main office, but no one else wearing similar outfits was sent out. I didn't go to the office that day, I went home, and missed the rest of school.

The next day the same teacher decided to confront the tension and constant conversations in the room about the dress code. She proceeded to say, "showing up half-nude and showing off your body is gross." Eyes immediately flashed to me because we all knew it was about me and my body. I wasn't going to tolerate her clear racism and attempts at shaming me, and responded to her that she was targeting girls of color. She didn't have an immediate response to this because I caught her off guard. After a few moments, she rambled her apologies. I told her, simply, that an apology was not what I was looking for; I wanted to see her realize her mistake and do something about it so that next time she would make a better decision. I offered the suggestion of taking an implicit bias test in order to face her bias against black people, and she agreed. The rest of the year I didn't have any more issues with her.

I appreciated that this one teacher was able to reflect on her actions and work to adjust, but that was just one teacher out of many in the school who were targeting black and brown students breaking the dress code. I knew that because of biases and the racism found in all other discipline policies, dress code would never be equally enforced unless racism, like, ended. Since immediately ending racism wasn't a plausible option, I wish it was, other students and I knew that the only other solution would be to either strip the dress code to the bare minimum, or to take it down all together. It was a process that took months, but I'm proud to say that the district officially has a dress code that makes it nearly impossible for students to be punished for their clothes unless they are breaking a nudity law or anti-discrimination policies.

Unfair discipline in schools affects students of color disproportionately compared to white students. I want to make a clear distinction about what I mean with the words, "punishment" and "discipline." Punishment, in the way I am using it, is a penalty used to discipline students. Discipline is the measures taken to have someone follow rules, act appropriately, and listen to instructions; it can involve punishment; however, I want to argue that discipline does not need to involve punishment, and there are more effective and fair ways to practice discipline. Therefore, when I use the words ineffective and unfair to describe discipline, I am referring to punishment.

Schools, being institutions upholding racism, criminalize black students the same way society does. The same way the black America population makes up most of the population of prisons, most students I see being suspended and expelled are black, and there is a correlation between the two that I will explore later. We are stereotyped in classes immediately the same way as we are stereotyped in society as wild, loud, troublemakers which makes teachers quick to punish us by calling security or getting administration involved. We are punished for things that we shouldn't be, and for things that white students get away with on a regular basis. The way students are unfairly disciplined can take many forms.

"My freshman year there was a white student who threatened to shoot up the school. He got suspended for three days. I got suspended for five days for calling him a school shooter on my Instagram account. Even though I did do something

wrong, my punishment was longer than a student who made a threat to kill people."

"In middle school during P.E. class some kids were making fun of me for supporting Hilary Clinton to run in the election. They started calling me names like 'baby killer' and other ones. They continued by ridiculing me for supporting Obama. I told the teacher, but instead of stopping them she interrogated me in front of the whole class on why I was a Democrat in the first place and why my family supported Obama. I was the only black person in the class, and she got me in trouble for people bullying me."

As I stated earlier, white students receive less of a punishment, or none, for the same or worse actions. It's another advantage that they have in school; they're able to get away with more without the fear of consequence. I've watched white students get away with cheating, plagiarizing, talking out of turn, being disrespectful, showing signs of violence and more. My freshman year, there was a boy two years older than me who posted a tweet, right before the school year started, that had side by side pictures of a woman in a burka and of a KKK member, and he captioned it "if they can wear their pillow cases, why can't I wear mine?" When students of color, and a few white students, at my school saw the tweet, they immediately called him out about how horrible what he said was. Instead of apologizing, he brushed it off as a joke. I'm not sure if it was his choice, or forced by administration, but he didn't attend the school that year. Only one year later, it was circulated around the school that he was returning, and people were mad about it. He was a known racist, and received no discipline that anyone knows of, and was even allowed to be the captain of the cross-country team. The fact that he was let off the hook shows the privilege white students have and the lenience they are granted.

Discipline is necessary in schools to keep people safe. If someone is a threat to the safety of themselves and others, or has acted in violent ways, it makes sense to remove them from the school until it is resolved. There are types of violence that need to be taken more seriously, especially gun violence, but smaller incidents should be handled differently. For instance, it's common at my school for students to get into physical fights. Usually, these students are black. It's easy to blame the students themselves for being violent at school, ridicule them for disregarding the safety of others, and then to have them suspended or expelled. But what is that really doing for anyone? The student is likely to continue using fighting to resolve problems. I believe that instead of simply kicking them out, they should be given the resources, support, and help needed for them to figure out a way to cope with the urges instead of acting on them during school. The goal should be to get the student back in the classroom as quickly as possible. It's more effective and beneficial for everyone involved to not punish the student, and to solve the problem through addressing the cause of the behavior.

Earlier I compared the criminalization of black students in schools to the criminalization of black people in society. I brought this up because black and brown kids who are unfairly disciplined and even expelled, end up dropping out which leads to the school-to-prison pipeline; a system in place that feeds students, almost exclusively students of color, into prison. Some people believe the pipeline is an unexpected consequence of policies in school, but I believe it's an intentional system where the government can exploit black and brown bodies for labor and continue to hold down communities of color for generations to come by locking up the youth.

In place of suspension, expulsion or detention for more serious incidents, schools should implement restorative justice policies. Restorative justice is way to resolve a situation by bringing those involved into a conversation to restore what has been broken, rather than using punitive methods to "fix" the problem. Its goal is to reconcile the situation between the people directly involved, and provide healing for the community. It leaves everyone feeling like they were heard, they matter, and they are wanted in the space. For restorative justice to work effectively and to make a change in the school's environment, it must be radically embraced in all aspects. It needs to be the foundation of discipline in the school. Instead of sending students who misbehave to security guards, they are sent to someone to talk to about what's going on, and provided help to get them back in the classroom. I'm not going to go too far in depth on this practice because I don't have experience with it, but I strongly believe that working with students instead of against them should be the basis for all discipline.

"With self-expression, I'm forced to tone everything down. I almost need to downplay my culture to be accepted. My school is strict on dress code. When a white girl

128

*wears something it's ok, but if I wear it it's
'out there' and stands out way more. I must
pretend to be someone who I'm not in order
to fit in or appease their conservative private
school values. I was afraid to get twists
because people would say, 'That's a pretty
ethnic style, you might want to lay off.'"*

*"I was kicked out of the class picture in
fifth grade for not having appropriate shoes
on; they were Jordan's. The teacher told
me they wouldn't be acceptable in the class
picture because they would stand out too
much, and when I said I would take them
off, they told me I would look poor with no
shoes on. So, no fifth-grade picture for me."*

I've learned over time that the "whiter" I present myself, the
less likely I will be unfairly disciplined. Everything from the way I
speak, to who I'm with, to what I wear, to the way my hair looks
affects the way that teachers and administration view me which
affects the way that they treat me. Schools are allowing racial biases
and stereotypes to affect discipline which teaches us that we need to
be whitewashed in order to not get in trouble. It's a harmful message
to be spreading because it only feeds into racist ideologies. When
black and brown students internalize these messages, it can cause us
to hate ourselves and feel the need to conform to white standards.
Beyond biases and stereotypes that are used against students of color,
unfair discipline can be seen within school policies.

Certain policies in schools target students of color directly.

Two specific policies from schools in Seattle, and in my high school, I want to call out are truancy and tardiness policies. Truancy refers to chronic absence of a student. I've been truant more than I haven't because of mental health issues that didn't qualify me for an excused absence. I've usually been able to talk my way out of it by proving that I was still able to maintain decent grades. This isn't the case for everyone. Schools can take students, and their parents, to court for truancy. Because the funding of the school is based on the level of attendance, it's in the school's best interest to keep students in attendance. Their solution to truancy is punishing the student and their parent for the absences. What is that really doing for anyone? There's no way to know that taking them to court will get them to improve their attendance, especially if the reason is out of control. A better way to handle truancy is for administration to talk with the students and their parents about what the issue is, and work together to create a plan that will result in a higher level of attendance. This solution is beneficial to both parties. The aspect of truancy policies that feeds into racism is that students who have an unstable homelife, live in poverty, are homeless, are in the foster care system, must support their families or deal with another adversity are the most likely to be truant. The people who face these adversities are usually people of color. None of these adversities are the student's fault, yet they have the blame cast on them and their family.

Penalizing tardiness has a similar issue. My school is an interesting example to look at in terms of tardiness. I go to school in a historically black neighborhood that has been gentrified. The school is known for its black culture and legacy, and is viewed as one of the best and most respected public schools in Seattle.

Unfortunately, due to gentrification, it is becoming more and more white. Many of the black people that attend the school live far away because they can no longer afford to live in the area. They often choose to attend the school because their family has attended for generations, they had to move during high school and didn't want to transfer, or they want to be involved in sports and activities that the school is known for. Since they live far away, they must commute, sometimes over an hour, to get to school. They can't control traffic, the public transit schedule, or other factors that could make them late, but get penalized for it. This is a difficult situation to explain to teachers and administration because technically they aren't allowed to attend the school if they don't live in the area. Because of the complexity of the factors in tardiness, I believe that schools should be more compassionate to students who are chronically late.

> *"I got in trouble a lot in Middle School. Partially because I didn't know how to act, but also because the system was against black students. I remember doing things like wiggling a pencil in math class and my teacher sent me to detention. White students always got away with the stuff I got in trouble for."*

I remember that when I was in kindergarten my teacher had a discipline policy in place that exemplifies how at a young age, kids of color are told they are "bad kids." The policy was simple in my eyes, if students were "good kids" who behaved in class and didn't get in trouble, they were free to walk with your friends whenever we left the classroom, but if they were a "bad kid" who misbehaved, they had to walk in a line with the other "bad kids" behind the teacher. Looking back, I remember how intense the shame was when I was labeled as a "bad kid." It didn't happen often to me because I was a stuck-up goody-two-shoes type of kid at that age, but there were kids in my class who were labeled as "bad" every single day. At such a young age, I can imagine how it would negatively affect their own beliefs of themselves, and if they get labeled as a "bad" every day, it makes sense that they would continue to play the role. My Kindergarten class was the only class in elementary school that was diverse because the honors program doesn't begin until first grade. I didn't make the correlation when I was five years old, but based off who I remember to be the "bad kids," I can say that the group was mostly kids of color.

Acknowledging and calling out poor behavior is one thing, but allowing it to define someone causes harm. Labeling it as "bad behavior" allows students to still see themselves as good people who are capable of being good, and only recognize the specific actions as bad. When it's a recurring issue that gets them in trouble every day, it's time for a conversation beyond "you are in trouble for being bad." Explaining to students of any age, even kindergarteners because they are people too, why their actions were wrong and allowing them to understand rather than punishing them without explanation is far more effective in the short and long term. When students are given specifics about what they need to change, they're more likely to make those changes than if they are punished for vague reasons. Listening to students is important in order to understand what the underlying cause is for their actions, and start working from there.

"Black people are being perpetuated in the media as causing a lot of the violence that's going on. I feel like that's more publicized with black people compared to white people. I think people at my school view black people like that too. The sophomore class went on a scavenger hunt one time. We were in Capitol Hill, a super nice neighborhood, a super safe neighborhood, and someone saw a black person, and I heard, 'Oh, this is getting sketchy.'"

The stereotypes that surround people of color in society follow them into school. Media is a huge factor in the way people think. Unfortunately, because of the way American society is set up, black and brown people are overly represented in the media as dangerous. This is one of the reasons why the school to prison pipeline has been so effective for oppression. It uses the prejudice that has been created in society against students of color in order to paint an image of them based off those stereotypes. When black students are assumed to be dangerous, any expression of anger is perceived as being violent and disobedient rather than an emotion. We learn to be careful of how we act, or we risk being perceived through the lens of stereotypes which can lead to discipline that doesn't fit the situation.

In eighth grade, my math teacher, kicked me out of class permanently for sitting at my desk and doing nothing. I was emerging from really struggling with mental health issues, and was now committed to getting my grades better, so I could move on to high school. It wasn't as simple as I hoped it would be, and especially in this class, I was having a tough time getting back on track and figuring out what the material was. My mom and I had filled him in on my situation, and at least in front of her, he seemed understanding. Whenever I tried to ask for help after that meeting, my teacher would refuse to answer my questions, and no one in my class would help me either. So, most of the time I had no idea how to do any of the work. I remember that I was sitting at my desk, not doing anything because I didn't know how to do anything, and he stormed over and yelled at me to get out, and stay out, of his class if I wasn't going to do the work. I tried to explain that I didn't know how to do the work because of how much I missed the last few weeks, and I needed help, but he dismissed everything I said. I was confused and frustrated because he wouldn't listen to me or help me, and clearly didn't care if I succeeded in the class, so I ended up leaving like he asked and never came back.

Looking back, this incident makes me disappointed in how quick many teachers and administration are to blame students of color for their failure. Instead of supporting their students when they're struggling, they punish us for it by sending us to administration, calling security on us, or kicking us out of the class. It puts the entire burden on the student, and those in power can give up on us without repercussions. Students slip through the cracks because no one is paying attention, or no one cares. There are alternatives to pushing students out of the classroom. Whether it's because of an academic failure, an altercation, or another reason, penalizing the student only keeps them away from an education. Accountability can make a huge difference in reducing unfair discipline. If authorities know that the student's point of view matters just as much as theirs, it can force them to question their actions. With racism being a major influence in the way people think and act, the current discipline policies allow students of color to be targeted. When teachers punish us or ignore us, it's hard to find somewhere in the school to get support. There is no way for students to stand up when they're being punished, and no system is in place where both students and authorities can hold each other accountable for their actions. I think one of the big reasons that accountability works is that it can turn a situation where a student is punished, to one where they are helped, and that should be the primary goal in discipline.

Spaces

My freshman year I heard about an upcoming trip held by a club at my school, the same one I was on staff Junior year, and signed up to go. I didn't know much about the trip except for that some of my friends had gone on the previous one and loved it. Retreats focus on looking at social and personal issues through racial lenses, building community, and personal growth. It includes various activities, forums, and an opportunity to share with the group about anything in one's life. There is something extremely intimate about these retreats that makes them so special.

Since I didn't know much about the trip beforehand, I didn't know what to expect; I didn't know if I should be excited, or if I would like it, so I planned to come in with an open mind. When I saw everyone who was going on the trip, my heart skipped a beat; there were so many students of color, and I wondered if this would be my chance to connect with them. I was going on the trip with two of my white friends, but after seeing all the other people there,

I knew I didn't want to spend much time with them. There were so many people who I desperately wanted to know, and become friends with. I was terrified about being rejected, but by the end of the first night of my first trip, I had found a place that I belonged. People wanted me to be there, and wanted to know me as much as I wanted to know them. I was shocked that for once, people wanted to hear my voice more than the voices of my white friends. I could talk about how insecure I've been about how I look my whole life and people listened to me. I could talk about how awful it was to be surrounded by whiteness my whole life, and how desperately I wanted more friends of color. People there didn't judge me; they understood me, and wanted to support me.

Throughout the weekend, I met people of color from my school who didn't take shit from anybody. They didn't care about catering towards white people or being friends with them, a completely new concept to me. White people were forced to acknowledge their inherent racism. It was clear to me that the space wasn't meant for them. White people were there, but not centered like I was accustomed to them being. In that space I had a break from caring about what white people think of me. I watched as people of color confidently corrected white people, and I stopped second guessing myself when I felt the need to speak up. I didn't feel worried about making anyone uncomfortable, or risking my safety, to say what I truly felt. The overall experience weekend changed my life. I came back to school with a different mindset. I wasn't going to put up with any shit from any white person again. Whatever space I was given, I would put up a fight. Going on this trip accentuated how white the other spaces in my life were, and I couldn't go back to only being in them. Once I got a taste of what a good space for me felt like, I needed to find more, which was another factor that pushed my involvement in other spaces of color.

Everyone is susceptible to being positively or negatively affected by the spaces that they're in the most. For kids and adolescents, school is one of the spaces we occupy the most, and therefore it's going to have some type of effect on us. We absorb the treatment we receive, the energy in the room, and the attitudes there and use that information to determine whether we enjoy being in that space. Because of all the negative experiences that I've accumulated at my school, my brain has labeled it as a negative space. In addition to what we absorb from the environment, schools are structured for white students to be successful and students of color to fail. Classes are structured for white students to do well with rules are in place that intentionally make getting through school more difficult for students of color. Every aspect of schools has been structured to be for the success of white students rather than for all students.

Overtime, my high school has become a dark place for me to walk into. The more I learned about institutionalized racism in the education system, the more I saw my school for what it was: a breeding ground for racism. I couldn't look at anything in the building anymore without seeing the racism within it. My eyes had opened to truly see the vast injustice within the school, and even though I'd noticed it before, it was now constantly in my face. I looked at things with a completely different lens that I had before, and the things that I saw were suffocating me. Especially throughout the process of interviewing for this book, it broke my heart to hear what my peers go through, and knowing that these experiences were based on systematic racism, and there wasn't much I could do, made me feel hopeless. From where I was standing, there was little good in the building, and things were just getting worse. As much as students have worked to make changes, we aren't heard or taken seriously by those in power. We try to create spaces where we feel safe, but maintaining those spaces with no support feels impossible. One of the hardest realizations that I had to face was that because of gentrification, the school was only going to get more and more white. The future of the school seems bleak, and as much as I want to fix it myself, I can't.

Aside from becoming more attuned to the racism, another big reason my school shifted into a negative space for me was because of personal events. During the winter of that year, after I was raped, things took a major turn. Not only was I traumatized from the rape itself, but the reaction that my boyfriend and close friends had made the experience much worse. They spent their time and energy trying to convince people that I was lying and to turn them against me. I was terrified of going back to the school and had nightmares about people harassing me, calling me a liar, and telling me I deserved it. I refused to enter the building for months after because I didn't think I would be safe. I eventually worked up to being able to go there for club meetings at lunch, but would only go if I had a friend to walk in with. Where I'm at now, I go to my high school building only when I absolutely must, and hate every single minute of it which is why I do full-time Running Start.

> *"I wish there was more room for girls of color. For me, I feel like I'm constantly stepping on someone else's space instead of feeling comfortable in class talking, or just walking around. I would make the*

classrooms more diverse to open space for people of color. School should have more education on 21st century norms because there is still so much ignorance."

One of the spaces that allows me to ground myself, and take off the mask I wear when I'm at my school building is Young Women Empowered (Y-WE). Sophomore year I was desperate to connect with communities of color and start my journey as a leader within activism. School wasn't a place where I could jumpstart that because it sucked out my soul every moment I was there. I was introduced to Y-WE by a family friend who was affiliated with the organization. Y-WE is an organization built to empower young women (including trans women, those assigned female at birth, and non-binary people) through mentorship, leadership building, and opportunities while centering the people of color in the space. I had no sense of what it was about beforehand, so she took me to the open house for me to get a feel for what it was all about. A few minutes into the open house, I knew I had found a good space. No one there had ever met me, yet I was still greeted as if I had been part of the community for years. I instantly felt welcomed by everyone in the room. I'd never felt this much radical love and warmth from a group of complete strangers before. I never wanted to leave the space; it felt like home.

I've been a part of the community for a few years now, and Y-WE has continued to be a welcoming and supportive space for me. I've grown as a person and as a leader through my participation in their programs. I've learned how to advocate for myself and others. When I came out as trans, they validated that identity. Having a space that I know I'm wanted in has showed me my worth as a person and that I deserve to feel valued by the people around me. I can go there as how I am, even when I'm not doing well, and know that I'll leave feeling at least a little better. I wish that I could find a place that makes me feel the same way in school, and even though I was able to find the support I needed outside of school, not everyone has access to or knowledge of other organizations.

> *"A safe place at school for me is the Y-scholar's office. Y-scholars is a program for black students so help us do our best in school. I really like Y-scholars because it's like a little family and I have support. A lot of teachers look at it negatively, which is weird, and I wish it wasn't like that."*

> *"White students are occupying spaces that aren't for them, they take up space and don't step back to allow students of color in. Teachers and other students sometimes don't care or notice that much. Not actively trying to have that diversity makes it toxic for students of color. AP and honors classes are toxic; we're isolated. Programs and clubs run by white students are not welcoming. The arts department is also a white space. Every space that's not a social justice program or athletics is not catered for students of color. There are clubs and programs at school for students of color, but the school system in general and classes don't provide safe spaces. The good*

spaces are created by students of color, so I don't
think the school is doing any of the work."

Some students have been able to find spaces within their schools that they feel safe in. From what I've noticed and heard from my peers, the safest places at school for students of color are the ones specifically created to be for students of color. When centering students of color isn't a clear goal, the default is for it to be a space for white students. Spaces for students of color that exist weren't there to begin with, and had to be created by students of color out of need. Clubs and extracurriculars are an important part of high school; they allow students to explore interests, make connections with people, and improve college applications. It continues to uphold racism when clubs aren't welcoming and comfortable for students of color by taking away these opportunities. I've had this experience trying out many clubs at my school, showing up and being the only black student in the room. If I manage to attend more than one meeting, I quickly see why there are no other black people there; the people running the club make it obvious that I'm not wanted. Especially academic clubs, such as Debate, Mock Trial, and more, tend to be filled with white students. Clubs focused around social justice and collectivizing are beneficial to be part of, they're my favorite clubs to be in, and provide tons of experiences and education on important issues, but the academic clubs at schools should also be serving students of color.

"I think going to a mostly non-white school
impacted me in a really good way. Because
of the students at my school, they've altered

the education for the audience. Being a person of color at a school of mostly people of color, I feel like I'm getting the best education possible. I'm not learning from a white person's perspective. The education is catered towards people of color. I don't know if that happens at other schools."

Schools where most students are people of color fosters a much different environment than schools with a substantial white population. When people of color are the primary group, the school can make shifts to be more accommodating for them without receiving backlash. I've never had the opportunity to be in a school where I wasn't the minority, or a school that actively fought against institutional racism. Imagining a school where those in power, not only the students, worked to improve the space for students of color, is something I often ponder. In my idea of this school, the teachers I have would represent a diverse background; I could look to them and see myself and my peers represented. The school would celebrate and support students who are passionate about making change. There would be open talks about racism and other systems during class time in order to fight racial ignorance. Racism and discrimination in any form would be shut down and condemned, and the perpetuators would be talked to by the teacher. Discipline would involve restorative justice and emphasize accountability. Teachers would be aware of their inherent biases, and shift them. I would be able to focus on doing well in my classes and learning rather than constantly fighting against the system because the administration and teachers would be doing their part to dismantle racism. It's important for me to envision what change would look like because it grounds me in my determination for change.

"As an Asian American woman, I've definitely been on the easier side of imbalance between white people and other people of color. I still think teachers, especially AP teachers, don't spend enough time in their classrooms trying to make people of color comfortable and instead they focus on making white students comfortable. This happens especially when topics such as racism and oppression are brought up, and instead of it being a learning opportunity for white students, they get protected from it."

"The faculty in school being majority white doesn't provide safe spaces for students of color to go to for help. White teachers can't provide the same help and protection as teachers of color can. Certain teachers don't hold belief that support students of color. Their classrooms are an unsafe space because they don't necessarily care. The worst spaces are in specific teacher's rooms."

Education should be provided equally across all students in a class which isn't naturally occurring, but teachers can work to create an environment that they want in a classroom. One class that stands out to me as doing an exemplary job at shifting away from a white space was my Asian Art History class that I took at my community college junior year. The teacher did a few key things in the beginning and throughout the class that allowed me to trust her and feel comfortable being a student of color in the room. On the first day of class, she immediately called out a problematic aspect of the class; it was called Asian Art History when we would only be learning about Japan, China, and India. Though this was a small gesture, it was important for the class to see she was open to critique. Another statement she made immediately was that the class would not tolerate any type of discrimination or hate towards any group. She made it clear that we could come to her with any concerns, and that she would take it upon herself to handle the problem. Aside from being explicitly welcoming to students of color, she also made sure that she was aware of everyone's pronouns, and the whole class knew how to refer to everyone in the room. These simple opening remarks set the tone for the rest of the quarter.

Later that quarter, when I was struggling with balancing school because of my mental health issues, I went to talk to her. It was one of the best decisions I made that quarter because I received more support from her than I ever had from other teachers. She made me feel like I mattered, and made it clear that she valued my health and safety more than my success in the class. Even if I was feeling terrible, if I needed a place to go, her classroom was always open. The class became a sanctuary for me, a place where I could feel safe. I know that if I ever need anything, she is someone who I can reach out to for help, and the trust I built with her over the span of the quarter is something I've never had with a teacher before.

I want school to be a good space for all students. I want school to be a space where people feel valued, safe, and supported.

I want to be able to leave school feeling enriched, not drained. Receiving education needs to be accessible to all students, and when the environment itself is toxic, it's not giving students a fair chance at success. Everything I've spoken on in this book has contributed to schools being a negative space for students of color. All the inequities, adversities, and harm that students of color face in school add up, bounce off each other, and weave together to create something evil. Schools have allowed the institutionalized racism to penetrate all aspects of the school, and continue to exacerbate the issue, rather than actively fight against it.

All the issues that I've spoken on throughout this book need to be addressed. Nothing is going to change if people aren't willing to do the work to make changes. Currently, the experiences of students of color are negative. We move through the system, knowing that it's one of the few ways to have opportunities in the future, and getting our education comes at a cost. I've had to sacrifice my well-being in order to do well in school. For years I've been forced to push my feelings to the side, and bottle everything up in order to get through my days. I've felt like a shell of myself for years, and I still haven't gotten all of myself back. The painful memories that I've accumulated throughout my time in the education system have affected me for years. As much as I wish I could say school has impacted me positively, the truth is that it hasn't. It failed me. I appreciate that I can get an education, but this isn't what it should be. I've never felt that my school has supported me, wanted me to succeed, or cared about my presence in the room. The suffocation I feel while attending has made me lose interest in my education, and I've been so close to giving up so many times, but I know that it's not an option for me to let the system take away my future.

The students who are subjected to attend school should be able to have a say in what they are subjected to. We have a voice, but we aren't heard. I'm tired of students of color and other marginalized students being dismissed, being stepped on and expected to stay strong the whole time. We are blamed for our struggles and failure while there are structural reasons causing our experiences. Everyone needs to really take a step back, and comprehend the meaning and the importance of the experiences we've had; something must change. Students need to have more power in an institution that is meant to serve us. Our input, stories, and requests need to be taken seriously because while we are in it, school is a huge part of our lives, and it continues to affect our lives for years. The atmosphere of school suffocates us, and we carry the weight of the experiences we've had on our shoulders. I want people to see that we deserve better, and we need to be fought for.

Conclusion

I started envisioning this book with the hope of making a change because I felt like I wasn't doing enough. I've been witness to the racism within the education system for my whole life, and wanted to speak out about it. The book started with a simple vision: interview students of color, and fill the space in between quotes with an analysis of what those experiences mean. I started writing the book several months later after countless interviews to find that I didn't really know what to write about. I had these quotes that I wanted to showcase, and I had my viewpoints, but it was missing something. As I forced myself to start writing, and see how it went, I kept thinking of more and more examples from my own life that illustrated the point I was trying to make. I was hesitant to put my own experiences in it; this book wasn't planned to be about me, it was about the education system through a lens of students of color. I came to understand that the fact that this book is not only about students of color, but also written by a current high school student of color, makes it unique to other books on similar topics.

Once I knew it was important to do, I tried to add in more about my own experiences throughout each chapter, and I really struggled with it at first. I was avoiding so many topics, so at first none of the stories carried the same weight on paper as they did in real life because I wasn't telling the full story, or giving the context. I was easily able to write about struggling academically, but avoided going into why I was struggling. I would mention an assignment that was inaccessible, but wouldn't explain why it was. I knew exactly what the narrative was lacking, but coming to terms with that took me a while.

Everyone has painful experiences, and I happen to have a lot of them. Keeping them separate from my experiences in school was impossible because of the way that they interacted with each other the whole time. There was no way for me to tell my story without really, truly, telling my story even though I don't like what it is. When I allowed myself to be honest with not only my future audience, but myself, that's when the real writing started to happen. The stories flowed out of me like they had been pushing to get out for years. As I allowed the memories to come back into my thoughts with full force, it was terrifying. Years of pain, shame, and misery washed over me with every single word I typed. I cried a lot during this process, about things I hadn't allowed myself to cry about for years. I would be writing in the office all day, holding myself together, and the second I got into my car and shut my door I would scream. I would scream for the younger versions of myself who didn't think their pain was valid, I would scream for the times I wish I had. Tears would rush down my face the whole drive home as I forced myself to process everything I had put into words that day. I allowed myself to feel the emotions that I avoided for so long. I don't exist as who I am today without those experiences; they've shaped me and my life for years. I spent a long time hating myself for the course my life has taken, from my eating disorder, to my grades, to being raped multiple times, and blamed myself for it all. Taking the time to write out these stories, and reflect on the factors within them, allowed me to start removing the blame from myself. If I could have a conversation with my any of my past selves now, I wouldn't want to blame them for the pain I carry today. I would hold them and tell them that everything will be ok, that they have to keep fighting, and that they deserve nothing but happiness. They don't deserve my hate, and I don't deserve my hate either.

I started this book to make a change and to shine a light on the experiences of students of color. As I worked on it, it morphed into something I had never imagined it being. At its foundation, this is a real look into the education system through the lens of students of color, and finding meaning out of those experiences. Instead of only finding meaning from other student's experiences, I was able to find meaning out of my experiences. I was able to find a way to turn these horrible, painful, stories into something that has a positive impact. My story is mine and mine only, but it speaks volumes about the impact of racism within the education system. The process of this was more than just writing a book, this was a process of self-reflection, acceptance, and healing for myself. I hope that after reading my stories, stories of other people of color, and what it all means, you feel connected to the issue. Whether you're a person of color who feels validated by these experiences, or if you're a white person who has gained empathy from them, I urge you to look into your past experiences, in and out of school, and find meaning out of them. Find something in your own life, or in the life of a loved one, that will motivate you to demand and fight for change. Connecting to our own reason is one of the first steps to collective action, and I hope you now want to make a change within our schools just as badly as I did when I started this book.

Azure Savage is a queer, trans, black high school student entering their senior year in high school. They live in Seattle with their mom, three dogs, and a cat. They hope to write things that make people think, reflect, and take action. Outside of writing, school, and community work, Azure spends time with friends, goes to hot yoga, and watches horrible movies for fun. Above all, Azure is a fighter. They aim to turn the painful experiences they've had into something positive by using them as a way to spread awareness, show people they're not alone, and improve the lives of others. They hope to continue work in community organizing, continue writing, and attend college for psychology after graduating high school. Eventually, they plan to pursue a career in trauma specialized psychology to help mental health patients struggling with trauma.